AF228636

Known primarily as a city of politicians and bureaucrats,
Washington, D.C. often gets a bad rap. But after living in the US capital
for seven years, covering the food, fashion and culture scenes,
I've watched the District grow, and can tell you that everything I love
about this place has absolutely nothing to do with what happens
in the government buildings downtown.

Plan to spend your days getting to know all that the charming,
historic neighborhoods away from the tourist areas have to offer,
and visiting engaging museums that aren't located on the National Mall.
If you're a foodie, you'll be thrilled with the variety here – this city
offers an incredible array of fantastic drinking and dining options,
which means you can spend your evenings savoring phenomenal
dishes prepared by world-class chefs.

D.C. has experienced a renaissance over the last few years,
and my once boring, stodgy town has gained new life – and a lot
of style. There are always new watering holes and eateries to try,
cerebral art exhibits to see and independent coffee shops and pop-up
events to check out. The people who've founded these businesses and
communities have made this a vibrant, quirky and exciting place to visit.

the hunt washington, d.c. writer

cori sue morris

Cori Sue Morris loves nights out at great new restaurants,
cocktails at the latest speakeasies, boutique fitness classes and
bottomless brunches. A high-energy entrepreneur, she's built a career
out of exploring Washington, D.C. and sharing her experiences on
bitcheswhobrunch.com, the website she co-founded. You can usually
find her at the corner table of her favorite coffee shop or
the best wine bar in town.

where to lay
your weary head
Rest up, relax and recharge
THE JEFFERSON

HOTEL TABARD INN
Cozy stay

1739 N Street NW (near 17th Street NW; near Dupont Circle)
+1 202 785 1277 / tabardinn.com
Double from $160

To me, the Hotel Tabard Inn is reminiscent of an English bed and breakfast. It even has a storied past: having opened in 1922, it once was a boarding house for women serving in the Navy during World War II. With its low ceilings, antique furniture and Old English-style appointments, you'll feel as if you've been transported to the early 1900s; the homey rooms even have the original keys. The restaurant here is exceptional and known for its famous brunch – particularly for the housemade doughnuts dipped in sugar and served with jam – and live jazz.

THE CARLYLE

Posh accommodation

1731 New Hampshire Avenue NW (near Riggs Place NW; Dupont Circle)
+1 202 234 3200 / carlylehoteldc.com

Double from $139

Located just off Dupont Circle NW on the quiet, tree-lined
New Hampshire Avenue, The Carlyle's guest rooms are sleek and
outfitted with flat-screen televisions, Tempur-Pedic mattresses
and high-quality bath products. Plus, the amenities are top-notch:
a fitness center, a yoga studio, in-room spa services and even
beds, bowls and mats for your furry friend. While the rooms are
contemporary, the hotel's dining establishment, The Riggsby,
is retro-glam, and has superb food and drinks.

THE EMBASSY ROW HOTEL

Modern convenience

2015 Massachusetts Avenue NW (near 21st Street NW; Dupont Circle)
+1 202 265 1600 / destinationhotels.com/embassy-row-hotel

Double from $179

Bright and zany, this pet-friendly hotel is located, as the
name mentions, on Embassy Row just north of Dupont Circle.
It's decorated with enormous hands as chairs, patterned wallpaper
and printed carpets, and has a rooftop pool, a bustling café
serving locally roasted coffee, snacks from D.C.-based companies
and an innovative eatery. This is a smart choice for those who
want their lodging to double as an activity center, as there's
a lineup of hotel-hosted events, including a DJ on Fridays,
weekend brunch, and rooftop yoga and parties during
the summer months.

THE GRAHAM GEORGETOWN

Upscale digs

1075 Thomas Jefferson Street NW (near M Street NW; Georgetown)
+1 202 337 0900 / thegrahamgeorgetown.com

Double from $295

If you prefer boutique hotels, The Graham Georgetown – located on an endearing side street along the C&O Canal, and a stone's throw from terrific shopping – is just the ticket. The 57-room hotel, with its gilded décor, dark corners, narrow hallways and stylish, state-of-the-art rooms, is très glam. What's more, there are two bars here: in the basement lies The Alex, a craft cocktail and small-plate dining concept that pays homage to scientist and inventor Alexander Graham Bell, and up on the roof you'll find The Observatory, where locals flock for sunset drinks.

THE JEFFERSON

Grandeur fit for a president

1200 16th Street NW (near M Street NW; Downtown)
+1 202 448 2300 / jeffersondc.com

Double from $325

When I'm in the mood for a staycation, my favorite getaway is The Jefferson, a light-filled, luxe hotel. Inspired by its namesake (yes, it's named after Thomas Jefferson), The Jefferson has sumptuous rooms inspired by the founding father's time in Paris and the design of his Virginia home, with high thread count linens, Italian marble bathrooms and smart technology in each room so that you can call housekeeping or request privacy by touching a button. The hotel also offers fine dining at Plume, which has a French-inspired menu, intimate nooks and wine cellars. The book room, which is filled with leather-bound tomes, is perfect for sipping a concoction by the fire from Quill, the hotel bar.

THE GRAHAM GEORGETOWN

logan circle

An inner-city residential neighborhood with Victorian architecture, amazing dining options and fantastic shopping, Logan Circle is my kind of city living – which is why it's the hood I call home. There's a plethora of diverse restaurants, buzzing drink joints with handcrafted beverages and independent boutiques filled with everything from little-known designer duds to rad antiques sourced at auction. Before all that, this thriving community housed army barracks during the Civil War. After the war came the ornate row houses, streetcars and parks, and the area now has two historic districts and a bevy of sites registered as landmarks. Delightful, notable and packed with both food and shopping, Logan Circle has it all.

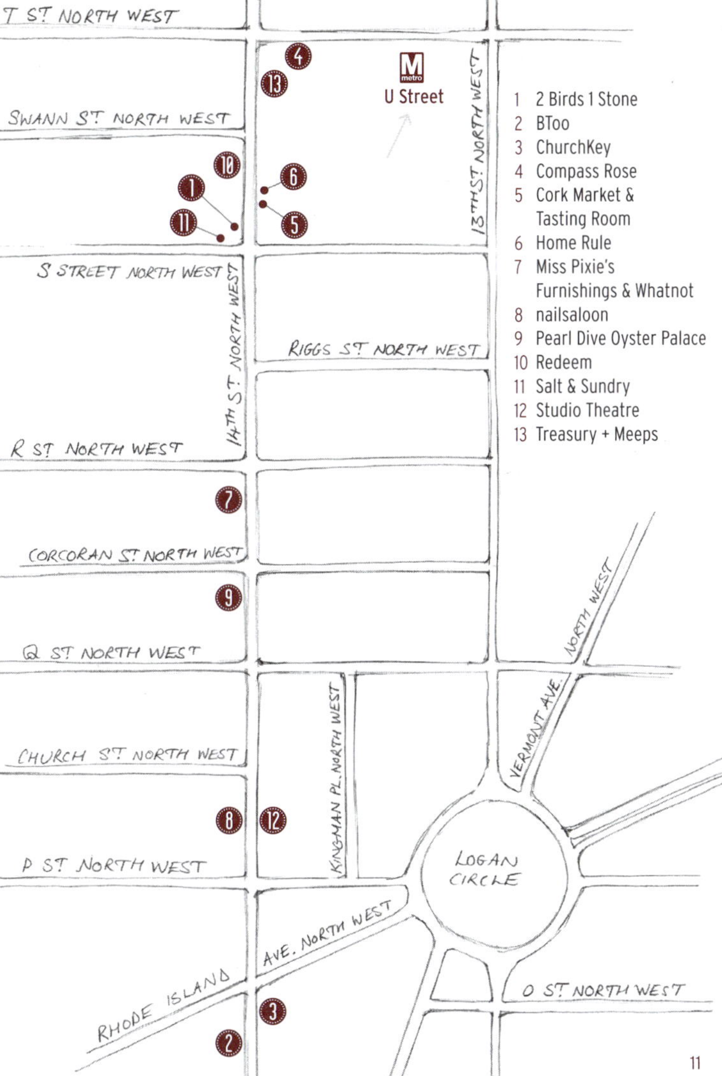

T ST NORTH WEST
SWANN ST NORTH WEST
S STREET NORTH WEST
R ST NORTH WEST
CORCORAN ST NORTH WEST
Q ST NORTH WEST
CHURCH ST NORTH WEST
P ST NORTH WEST
RIGGS ST NORTH WEST
14TH ST NORTH WEST
13TH ST NORTH WEST
KINGMAN PL NORTH WEST
VERMONT AVE. NORTH WEST
RHODE ISLAND AVE. NORTH WEST
O ST NORTH WEST
LOGAN CIRCLE
M metro
U Street
1 2 Birds 1 Stone
2 BToo
3 ChurchKey
4 Compass Rose
5 Cork Market & Tasting Room
6 Home Rule
7 Miss Pixie's Furnishings & Whatnot
8 nailsaloon
9 Pearl Dive Oyster Palace
10 Redeem
11 Salt & Sundry
12 Studio Theatre
13 Treasury + Meeps

RECOMMENDED BY
BRENT KROLL
WINE DIRECTOR OF NEIGHBORHOOD RESTAURANT GROUP

2 BIRDS 1 STONE

Intimate lounge with bespoke drinks

**Lower Level, 1800 14th Street NW (near S Street NW) / No phone
2birds1stonedc.com / Closed Sunday and Monday**

2 Birds 1 Stone is a slick, subterranean bar with a lively atmosphere. The chic, all-white space has snug booths, ideal for gossiping with friends or cuddling up on a date. Of course, the real draw here is the beverage program: the hand-drawn menu, illustrated with wacky cartoons, changes weekly. If I'm not feeling anything they're touting that week, I'll ask the bartender to mix me something whiskey-based, as they're happy to whip up a drink suited to your particular tastes. The speakeasy shares ownership with its upstairs neighbor, Doi Moi, which is an excellent place for dinner.

BTOO

Decadent Belgian cuisine

1324 14th Street NW (near Rhode Island Avenue NW)
+1 202 627 2800 / btoo.com / Open daily

Waffles are the name of the game at this high-end dining room owned by chef Bart Vandaele, who hails from Belgium. You can witness him and his team making everything from pastry dough to sausages in the open kitchen. You may be thinking, "Didn't you mention waffles?" I did. There are dozens of both sweet and savory varieties. My picks are the wafel van kreeft with Maine lobster, radishes, lobster bisque and a salad, and the fried apple variation topped with caramel sauce as well as speculoos cookie ice cream for dessert. If waffles aren't your thing, you can rest easy knowing there are offerings like truffle foie gras with figs; mushroom risotto; and slow-cooked pork belly with radishes and ramps to sate your palate.

CHURCHKEY

Pints and flatbreads

1337 14th Street NW (near Rhode Island Avenue NW)
+1 202 567 2576 / churchkeydc.com / Open daily

At the dawn of the microbrew craze, Vermont was the place to be, and it's where Greg Englert, ChurchKey's beverage director, showed early aptitude as a beer sommelier. This gastropub has hundreds of choices available, including 100 drafts: the selection can definitely be overwhelming. Blessedly, you can order a tasting size to try the many (many) varietals, from crisp to hoppy and silky to earthy. Each brew pairs well with the inspired pub grub, such as confit duck leg or fig and prosciutto flatbread. Delight in your choice, enjoy the view from the floor-to-ceiling windows and give thanks that the craft craze is still going strong.

COMPASS ROSE

Local tavern, global flavor

1346 T Street NW (at 14th Street NW) / +1 202 506 4765
compassrosedc.com / Open daily

Opened by a globetrotting couple who visited 30 countries between 2009 and 2012, Compass Rose specializes in international street food. Nestled in a narrow space, the interior is decorated like a Moroccan hostel, with wooden benches, mismatched Arabian throw pillows and star lanterns hanging from the ceiling. The mixed drinks are creative and there's a standout list of artisanal beers, as well as a rotating menu of fare from South America, Europe and the Middle East, like arepas filled with braised lamb, smoky poblano salsa and Cotija cheese; Greek-style grilled calamari with oregano, mint, lemon, garlic and chili oil; Jamaican goat curry; and Spanish patatas bravas. If it's available, you must order the khachapuri, an enormous Georgian bread filled with cheese and topped with an organic egg and butter.

CORK MARKET & TASTING ROOM

Small-batch wines and cheeses

1805 14th Street NW (near S Street NW) / +1 202 265 2675
corkdc.com / Open daily

Diane Gross was five years old when she had her first wine experience: stomping grapes in a barrel. Though the vintage bombed, it didn't dampen her enthusiasm for the drink. Diane has a wealth of knowledge when it comes to the temperamental grape, and at Cork Market & Tasting Room she sources an impressive assortment from vintners who know what they're doing. I've found you can have an extraordinary experience here just by browsing the Champagne case, but I can also wax on about the fromage and the chocolates. When a sunny day inspires a picnic, swing by here to fill a basket with some incredible fixings, including their scrumptious fried chicken and, of course, a perfect bottle of vino.

HOME RULE

Super organized décor stop

**1807 14th Street NW (near S Street NW) / +1 202 797 5544
homerule.com / Open daily**

This bright, compact housewares shop is anything but traditional. It's filled with funky yet helpful items for your abode – particularly the kitchen. The mission of Home Rule is to stock items that are distinct, useful and well-priced, and the store excels at this. You can find humorously shaped ice cube trays and colorful zesters, as well as a surfeit of kitchen appliances I never knew I needed but can no longer live without. It's an outstanding place to find a present for anyone who cooks, drinks or enjoys an orderly home. My go-to gift for everyone, from a friend's housewarming to my aunt who is impossible to shop for, are the dish towels printed with the D.C. metro map.

MISS PIXIE'S FURNISHINGS & WHATNOT

Vintage home goods emporium

1626 14th Street NW (near R Street NW) / +1 202 232 8171
misspixies.com / Open daily

Pixie Windsor's business philosophy is this: handpick the most desirable household objects at auctions, bring them back to her charming store and sell them to those lucky enough to stop by that week. Looking for antiques? Miss Pixie's has them. Need a whimsical piece of art to adorn your living room? I've seen a pop-art portrait of a luchador for sale. Once you're inside, don't be surprised to find yourself lusting after a cool mid-century couch, coffee table or lamp. If you're the type that needs to be the first to find the good stuff, then drop by on Wednesday, as that's when Pixie's latest finds go on the floor. Happy hunting!

NAILSALOON

Manicures and cocktails

2nd Floor, 1508 14th Street NW (near P Street NW)
+1 202 299 0095 / thenailsaloon.com / Open daily

RECOMMENDED BY **MEG BIRAM** FOUNDER OF MEGBIRAM.COM

I believe that getting your nails done should never be another task on your to-do list, but rather an appointment that feels like a reward. As the name implies, nailsaloon is a twist on your typical nail salon in that it serves complimentary booze (or coffee or tea, if you prefer). You'll usually find me here on Fridays, when I scoot up to the second floor and relax into a plush leather seat next to a girlfriend for a pedicure and a glass of wine. Co-owned by two best friends, they're all about girl power and giving back – a portion of the proceeds benefits local women's charities. The space is incredibly clean and the polishes are non-toxic, which means that you won't be able to get a gel manicure, but don't fret – your mani or pedi will be long-lasting, and you'll have a fabulous time.

PEARL DIVE OYSTER PALACE

A shucking good time

1612 14th Street NW (near Corcoran Street NW) / **+1 202 319 1612**
pearldivedc.com / **Open daily**

A meal at Pearl Dive Oyster Palace is what its name suggests: a plunge into a wonderfully appetizing world, and I say jump right in, the water's fine. Varietals of oysters from Chincoteague to Hama Hama to Rappahannock will have you swimming in a sea of glee. Jeff Black's New Orleans-inspired joint not only serves the briny wonders, but also has Creole staples like Andouille sausage and tomatoes, and refreshing libations, such as the Pearl Cup (Pimm's, gin, cucumber, lime, mint and housemade ginger beer). When you've stuffed yourself silly and resurface for air, you'll feel fully satisfied – and will be shocked when you step outside and into Washington, D.C. instead of Nola's Bourbon Street.

REDEEM

Threads from up-and-coming designers

**1810 14th Street NW (near Swann Street NW) / +1 202 332 7447
redeemus.com / Open daily**

One of the city's only remaining independently owned clothing shops, Redeem is a minimalistic men's and women's boutique. You'll find quality emerging brands like Assembly New York, Native Danger, House of 950 and Misanthrope, alongside gloriously scented candles from Virginia-based Sydney Hale Company and delicate silver and gold jewelry from local designer Sophie Blake. The wares are pricey – think $200 black T-shirts – but I like dropping in when I need a few wardrobe basics and know I want items that will last. Plus, I get a thrill out of supporting homegrown shops and under-the-radar fashion names.

SALT & SUNDRY

Well-curated lifestyle boutique

1401 S Street NW (at 14th Street NW) / +1 202 621 6647
shopsaltandsundry.com / Open daily

You could spend hours in tiny Salt & Sundry. Inspired by the owner's love for impeccable hospitality and gatherings, this store has an ever-changing supply of goods for living the good life, including barware, Martini and highball glasses, linens, throw pillows, Moroccan poufs, handcrafted furniture and more. There's also jewelry from D.C.-based designers like Mallory Shelter, accessories (including a handmade clutch I've had my eye on), candles and paper goods. With a careful focus on high-quality, made-in-America goods and thoughtful accents, you'll be hard-pressed to leave without spending a pretty penny.

STUDIO THEATRE

Bringing the drama

**1501 14th Street NW (near P Street NW) / +1 202 332 3300
studiotheatre.org / Open daily**

With its name in bright lights, Studio Theatre is a Logan Circle landmark, and has been a leader in D.C. theater for nearly 40 years. The enormous, four-level space hosts some of the most noteworthy playwrights in the nation, and mounts award-winning shows as well as experimental works by gifted emerging writers each season. Past productions include *Bloody Bloody Andrew Jackson*, an irreverent musical that imagines the controversial American president as a rock star, *Bachelorette* by Leslye Headland, which later became a film, and Tom Stoppard's *The Real Thing*. What's more, ticket prices are affordable: $25 for those under 30; otherwise between $30 and $70. They also serve wine, and often throw fun pre- and post-show parties.

TREASURY + MEEPS

The District's top retro shop

2104 18th Street NW (near California Street NW) / +1 202 265 6546
shoptreasury.com / Open daily

In this government town where a suit any color other than blue is considered somewhat risqué, an impeccable collection of vintage clothing is not the first thing that comes to mind when someone says Treasury. But Treasury is the choice venue for men's and women's pre-loved threads. The styles range from cool and hip to totally unusual, like '80s football jackets, skinny ties, plumed fascinators and loads of snazzy footwear like platform sandals and clogs. Personally, I like mulling through the accessories and '60s go-go dresses. Now that Treasury has combined with throwback boutique and costume store Meeps, it's the prime destination for shoppers looking for something a little different.

The boozier, the better

BAR CHARLEY

1825 18th Street NW (near Swann Street NW;
Dupont Circle), +1 202 627 2183, barcharley.com
weekend brunch, 10am–3pm

CENTRAL MICHEL RICHARD

1001 Pennsylvania Avenue NW
(near 11th Street NW; Penn Quarter), +1 202 626 0015
centralmichelrichard.com
Sunday brunch, 11am–2:30pm

HANK'S ON THE HILL

633 Pennsylvania Avenue SE (near 7th Street SE;
Capitol Hill), +1 202 733 1971, hanksoysterbar.com
weekend brunch, 11am–3pm

LAVAGNA

539 8th Street SE (near G Street SE; Capitol HIll)
+1 202 546 5006, lavagnadc.com
weekend brunch, 10am–2:30pm

TED'S BULLETIN

505 8th Street SE (near E Street SE; Logan Circle)
+1 202 544 8337, tedsbulletin.com
open daily, all-day breakfast

Washingtonians take brunch very seriously: it's not just a meal, but a social function with a culture all its own. By and large, brunch is only served on weekends, but there are a few places that get in on the action during the week as well. I'm a girl who loves brunch so much I put it in my website's name, and these are a few of my top spots for noshing in the capital.

The midday meal can be casual and inexpensive, like at **Bar Charley**, a hole-in-the-wall that serves up any Southern-inspired entrée and free-flow drinks for less than $25. My usual is the chicken and waffles – it's worth the small upcharge – and you sure won't want to miss the cinnamon rolls. For a more refined bottomless experience, hit up **Central Michel Richard** on a Sunday to get a taste of what the eponymous James Beard Award-winning chef has to offer.

My go-to is **Lavagna**, a reliable little Italian place on Barracks Row in Capitol Hill that dishes up delectable, fresh fare, a deal on endless drinks, and a warm, laid-back atmosphere. Though everything is great, I adore the Nutella pancakes, mushroom risotto and chocolate pot de crème.

The best place for kids or kids-at-heart is **Ted's Bulletin**. It seems apt to compare it to Willy Wonka's Chocolate Factory since it serves homemade versions of Pop Tarts, doughnuts and assorted sugar-laden confections. For those without a sweet tooth, there are savory options like soups and grilled cheese sandwiches. Though the family-friendly diner has opened a few locations around town, the original is in Capitol Hill. Don't forget to order a spiked milkshake.

Speaking of booze, the alcoholic cereal at **Hank's on the Hill** is one of the many reasons the seafood joint is worth a visit. (I told you Washingtonians take brunch seriously!) In the warm months, I'd advise grabbing a seat on the patio and staying a while. Begin your meal with a Bloody Mary and some oysters, continue with a bowl of alcohol-infused Cinnamon Toast Crunch, then move on to a lobster roll with Old Bay fries for the main event.

shaw

I spend most of my days – and nights, for that matter – in Shaw, an area with a rich history: it was originally an encampment of freed slaves that later became an African-American intellectual and cultural center. Need proof? Before decamping to Harlem, Langston Hughes and Duke Ellington called this neighborhood home. Nowadays, Shaw is primarily residential, lined with darling Victorian-style homes. Over the last few years, it's been undergoing a transformation and has seen bars, restaurants and coffee shops pop up, and then go on to be some of the hippest and most acclaimed places in the city. From the only District-based coffee roaster to an eclectically decorated en plein air beer garden, to some of the city's top cuisine, this is an up-and-coming enclave bursting with promise.

1 Atlantic Plumbing Cinema (off map)
2 Barber of Hell's Bottom
3 Chaplin's Restaurant
4 Compass Coffee
5 Convivial
6 Dacha Beer Garden
7 JRINK
8 Lettie Gooch (off map)
9 The Dabney
10 The Royal (off map)
11 Typecase Industries (off map)
Shaw-Howard U
metro
S ST NORTH WEST
R ST NORTH WEST
RHODE ISLAND AVE NORTH WEST
Q ST NORTH WEST
9TH ST NORTH WEST
8TH ST NORTH WEST
7TH ST NORTH WEST
MARION ST NORTH WEST
6TH ST NORTH WEST
5TH ST NORTH WEST
P ST NORTH WEST
O ST NORTH WEST
N ST NORTH WEST
10TH ST NORTH WEST
BLAGDEN ALLEY NW
M ST NORTH WEST

ATLANTIC PLUMBING CINEMA

Indie flicks and a full bar

807 V Street NW (near 8th Street NW) / +1 202 534 1965
landmarktheatres.com/washington-d-c/atlantic-plumbing-cinema
Open daily

I'm a sucker for a Friday night movie, and adore Atlantic Plumbing Cinema, which has an upmarket, adult atmosphere. Housed in the mixed-use Atlantic Plumbing development that includes apartments, dining options and local vendors like Typecase Industries (see pg 41), the theater has retained the industrial aesthetic. Within the cinema, there's a bar and lounge area near the concession stand that serves booze and food, and it exclusively shows independent films. Plus, it's located at the nexus between D.C.'s two most buzzing neighborhoods, U Street and Shaw, making it easy to move on to a slinky jazz club or happening watering hole if you don't want to call it a night after your film.

BARBER OF HELL'S BOTTOM

Hip grooming for dapper dudes

818 Rhode Island Avenue NW (at 9th Street NW)
+1 202 332 0200 / barberofhellsbottom.com / Closed Sunday

Operating under the credo, "Fine cuts and luxurious shaves for today's gentlemen," this is a barbershop that takes hair seriously, with services ranging from stellar haircuts and straight razor shaves to beard trimming, coloring services and gray blending. You can spot a guy who's a regular here from a mile away: you'll know these gents by the clean lines and well-groomed beards, and will see them all over Shaw. A visit to this old-school-style barber is a necessary experience for the modern man – but know that this isn't a quick appointment; be sure to allow sufficient time for the tattooed stylists to work their magic.

CHAPLIN'S RESTAURANT

Prohibition Era hooch and noodle bowls

1501 9th Street NW (near P Street NW) / +1 202 644 8806
chaplinrestaurantdc.com / Open daily

This sexy cocktail bar-meets-noodle shop is vampy in the best possible way: the dark space has a red-and-black color palette that feels oh-so Old Hollywood glam. An ode to the comedian Charlie Chaplin, this bi-level Japanese eating house is the type of place where I can get an enormous serving of ramen, a tremendous Old Fashioned and complimentary serve-yourself popcorn that comes in several different flavors – aka the type of place I love. As for food, you'd be wise to order the bite-sized pork dumplings and the filling Chaplin A.S.S., a sweet-and-spicy red curry with lemongrass, coconut milk and pork butt chashu. The outside patio is enormous, heated in the colder months and pet-friendly, making it popular regardless of the season.

COMPASS COFFEE

Locally roasted beans

1535 7th Street NW (near Q Street NW) / No phone
compasscoffee.com / **Open daily**

Washington's only local roaster, Compass Coffee is run by two former Marines whose goal upon coming home was to open a place that provides no-fuss "real good coffee," as well as pastries and tea, to the people of their hometown. On any given day, this café is packed with young professionals, families and friends working and socializing. Aficionados can enjoy a fair trade, single-origin pour-over or espresso at the bar while watching the roasting process, and novices can learn about different blends from the affable baristas. Warning: the nitro cold brew is addictive.

CONVIVIAL

French-American dining

801 O Street NW (at 8th Street NW) / +1 202 525 2870
convivialdc.com / Open daily

With a lively atmosphere, plates made to share and craft beverages aplenty, Convivial takes its name to heart. The polished venue has colorful accents and serves up gourmet, French-inspired American sustenance. I'm lucky enough to call well-respected chef Cedric Maupillier a friend, but I swear I'm not being biased when I say I can't get enough of his thick accent and imaginative recipes. My must-eats are the leeks dijonnaise, the cured arctic char with taramasalata, apple and elderberry dye, and the much lauded fried chicken "coq au vin," which has been dubbed the tastiest poultry in town by critics.

DACHA BEER GARDEN

Drink from a boot at this outdoor oasis

1600 7th Street NW (at Q Street NW) / +1 202 350 9888
dachadc.com / Open daily, March to December

The enormous portrait of Elizabeth Taylor and the line around the block make Dacha Beer Garden impossible to miss. From March to December, the al fresco, animal-friendly space is packed with those who gather on communal picnic benches for happy hour with friends old and new. Not afraid to break from tradition, there are no lederhosen-clad servers offering table service here: you'll have to order at the bar from the vast selection of German, Belgian and American artisanal brews. Beer not your thing? Choose from the list of wines, meads and ciders. When you get hungry, there are traditional pretzels and schnitzels, and not-so-traditional, but oh-so-delish fried pickles to sate your appetite.

JRINK

JRINK

Fresh-pressed vegetable juices

**1228 Blagden Alley NW
(near M Street NW)
+1 202 289 0044**
jrinkjuicery.com / Open daily

It's hard to tell what I love more: the delightful green concoctions, or the beautiful branding and pop-up locations from JRINK, a women-led juicery with a handful of small outfits across the city. I fuel up after the gym and while shopping – which, the way I do it is basically the same as going to the gym – with the Build Me Up, a creamy, protein-packed beverage made with almonds, vanilla, cinnamon and dates, and I cleanse after a night out with the Clean Me Up 3, which combines burdock root, green apple, pineapple, ginger, cayenne pepper and turmeric. Delicious and nutritious.

LETTIE GOOCH

Fun outfits to shake it up

1921 8th Street NW, Suite 110 (near T Street NW) / +1 202 332 4242
lettiegooch.com / Open daily

It's amazing what a good dress can do for a girl. With a smidge of effort and five minutes to spare, a well-designed frock and a sharp pair of shoes can turn frump into fabulous. Incidentally, five minutes is about how long it takes to find something divine in Lettie Gooch, a women's boutique with an old-fashioned name, but nary a matronly shift in sight. This store happily nudges the ladies of D.C. out of their fashion-conservative boxes. Owner Teresa Watts wouldn't have to ask me twice to jump into a form-flattering sheath that forgives the "eat" side of this job. Though you'll find a wide variety of clothing here, it's no slouch in the accessories department, either.

THE DABNEY

Farm-to-table eats

122 Blagden Alley NW (near M Street NW) / +1 202 450 1015
thedabney.com / Closed Monday

An unmarked wooden farmhouse door in Blagden Alley distinguishes
the entrance to The Dabney, a cozy restaurant with a rustic-chic setting.
The low lighting and open kitchen help to create one of the most
stunning eateries in the city; as such, it's my top choice for celebrations,
date nights and impressing out-of-town guests. While the New American
menu changes with the seasons, I always order whichever regionally
sourced vegetable is currently available and conclude my meal with the
rye blondie topped with buttermilk ice cream, a decadent finale that's
fitting for the vibe.

THE ROYAL

South American flavors

**501 Florida Avenue NW (near 5th Street NW) / +1 202 322 7777
theroyaldc.com / Open daily**

You can spend an entire day in The Royal, a coffee shop by day and bar by night located in the heart of LeDroit Park. Named for the building's previous life as the former Royal Liquor Store, this venue is inspired by its owners' Colombian heritage, and serves up arepas, empanadas and choripán (housemade chorizo on toasted bread). If you can't afford to set up shop here for a whole day, go for breakfast and enjoy my choice, the matcha latte (which is worth the trip alone) or swing by in the evening to tuck into a cheese-filled corn arepa and an artisanal libation; the vermouth is made in-house and definitely worth a taste.

TYPECASE INDUSTRIES

Quirky paper goods

**2122 8th Street NW (near V Street NW) / +1 202 827 5834
typecaseindustries.com / Closed Monday**

I'm the type of girl who still sends handwritten notes, and I never want
my stationery to be boring or predictable. When my supply needs to be
refreshed, I hightail it to Typecase Industries, a letterpress shop located
in the Atlantic Plumbing complex (see pg 30), where I can find a greeting
card to fit every single friend in my life, from bright and sweet thinking-of-
you sentiments to off-color salutations that are sure to make the receiver
laugh, and maybe even blush. This emporium stocks everything from
cards to coasters to T-shirts, and offers custom design services if you want
something bespoke. Stop by to purchase some kicky cards and writing
materials, or sign up for a workshop to learn how to DIY.

get cultured

Unique homes of art and history

Thanks to the Smithsonian Institution, Washington boasts 19 free museums, most of which are located on tourist central: the National Mall. Skip the Hope Diamond, Betsy Ross's American flag and the very long lines, and instead head to the impressive displays at these lesser-known, less crowded art spaces.

The Phillips Collection is America's first modern art museum, and its permanent collection houses several works from such international greats as Henri Matisse, Georgia O'Keeffe, Pablo Picasso and Vincent van Gogh. On the first Thursday of each month, the museum stays open late to host its after-hours series, which includes gallery talks, live music and drinks; one of my favorite activities for friend dates.

Known as the home of the presidential portraits, **National Portrait Gallery** is more than just heads of state: it boasts an amazing array of photography and portraits from the last several centuries. I love the 20th-century assemblage, which showcases stunning images of Audrey Hepburn, the Beatles and other pop culture icons. It also brings in stimulating exhibits, with past shows including street artist Shepard Fairey's *Hope* (the famous Obama poster) and *Staging the Self*, a look at present-day portraiture.

Even if you aren't an art lover, the **Hirshhorn Museum and Sculpture Garden** is fun. Its offbeat, in-your-face exhibits – such as a display of Surrealist sculpture, and a show made up of rarely or never-before-seen early- to mid-20th-century Italian art – make this one of my preferred spots to spend hours on end.

HIRSHHORN MUSEUM AND SCULPTURE GARDEN
700 Independence Avenue SW (near 7th Street SW; National Mall), +1 202 633 4674, hirshhorn.si.edu
open daily

NATIONAL PORTRAIT GALLERY
8th and F Streets NW (Penn Quarter)
+1 202 633 8300, npg.si.edu, open daily

NEWSEUM
555 Pennsylvania Avenue NW (near 6th Street NW; Penn Quarter), +1 202 292 6100, newseum.org
open daily

RENWICK GALLERY
1661 Pennsylvania Avenue NW (near 17th Street NW; Downtown), +1 202 633 1000
renwick.americanart.si.edu, open daily

THE PHILLIPS COLLECTION
1600 21st Street NW (near Q Street NW; Dupont Circle), +1 202 387 2151, phillipscollection.org
closed Monday

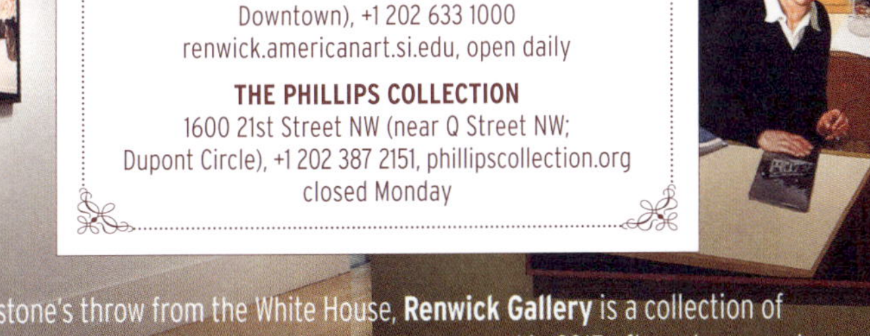

A stone's throw from the White House, **Renwick Gallery** is a collection of contemporary craft and decorative arts. It reopened in 2015 after a large-scale renovation, and did so with panache by mounting *Wonder*, a buzzworthy, multi-artist show that played with light and texture to totally immerse visitors in the art.

For something a little different, swing by **Newseum**, which is dedicated to the history of news. The permanent collection has something for everyone, with lighter exhibits on sports and presidential pets, and harder-hitting subjects featuring coverage of September 11, 2001 and Hurricane Katrina. Be sure to check out the newspaper gallery lined up out front – it displays a front page of a paper from each US state, and changes daily.

penn quarter

The busy, bustling Penn Quarter neighborhood lies alongside downtown, close to the National Mall, and is home to the Verizon Center, where The Wizards and The Capitals play, and where major concerts take place. As a result, the hood is always jam-packed with jersey-clad sports fanatics and eclectic crowds jazzed to see a beloved musician. Don't let that deter you. A destination for foodies, there's an incredibly high concentration of phenomenal dining experiences in this area. You'll find world-class cuisine from well-respected chefs that will have gourmands clamoring for a seat, boundary-pushing theater and intriguing museums like the National Portrait Gallery and Newseum (see page 42), making this community one that you shouldn't miss.

1 China Chilcano
2 Daikaya
3 Denson Liquor Bar
4 Graffiato
5 Mandu (off map)
6 Rasika
7 Red Apron Butcher
8 Woolly Mammoth Theatre
H ST. NORTH WEST
G ST. NORTH WEST
6TH ST. NORTH WEST
metro
Gallery Place-Chinatown
F ST. NORTH WEST
metro
Judiciary Square
E ST. NORTH WEST
STREET
WEST
7TH ST. NORTH
8TH ST. NORTH
5TH ST. NORTH
D ST. NORTH WEST
WEST
metro
Penn Quarter Station
INDIANA AVE. NORTH

CHINA CHILCANO

Fusion food from D.C.'s most famous cuisinier

418 7th Street NW (near D Street NW) / +1 202 783 0941
chinachilcano.com / Open daily

What the capital lacks in celebrities, it makes up for with chefs and politicians. Chef José Andrés is undoubtedly the personality (and he has a big one) with the largest following. His newest concept, China Chilcano, is inspired by Peruvian cuisine, which has strong Japanese and Chinese influences. The décor incorporates those themes, too. There's a brightly painted mural, hanging red lanterns and printed throw pillows. Large parties are seated at low Japanese-style tables – word to the wise, don't make the mistake of wearing a skirt. When it comes to ordering, I recommend the pisco sour, and sampling a little of everything: ceviches, sashimi, dim sum and authentic Peruvian mainstays like chaufas (fried rice) and lomo saltado, a beef stir-fry. Fancy something sweet? The chocolate snail will do you nicely.

DAIKAYA

Nippon-style eats and drinks

705 6th Street NW (near G Street NW) / +1 202 589 1600
daikaya.com / Open daily

Daikaya is a two-level experience: ramen shop downstairs and Asian small plates upstairs. As I can't resist a well-made drink, I normally head right to the dark, alluring long bar with decorative accents both serious (Japanese shodo) and playful (wacky cats). The beverage list boasts a strong selection of sake and Japanese whiskies, as well as house specialities, like a twist on a Moscow Mule – think vodka, peach and ginger beer – and The Theory of Moral Sentiments, created with Great King Street Glasgow scotch, Chauffe Coeur brandy, cinnamon honey, and Lindera Farms wild ginger vinegar. As for tackling the menu, my tactic is to order some veggies (the fried garlic and the chilled cucumbers are my picks), as well as some beef and chicken skewers and onigiri.

DENSON LIQUOR BAR

D.C.'s sexiest cocktail joint

**600 F Street NW (at 6th Street NW) / +1 202 499 5018
densondc.com / Closed Sunday**

With its dim lighting and magnificent Art Deco glamour — black-and-white geometric tiles, black leather booths with sleek gold trim and an enormous backlit bar — Denson Liquor Bar is worthy of Jay Gatsby himself. Much like a speakeasy, you must turn off a busy street and head downstairs to access this bar, which serves Prohibition-style booze and light bites. The drinks aren't the predictable Manhattan or Martini, though. Instead, there are artisanal concoctions like the Fall in Waverly Place, made with apple brandy, bourbon, Benedictine and bitters, and the Tolstoy, featuring vodka, pear liqueur and lemon juice. My drink of choice here is the Modern Cocktail #3: bourbon, sloe gin, lemon juice, simple syrup and plum bitters.

GRAFFIATO

Jersey-Italian flavor

707 6th Street NW (near G Street NW) / +1 202 289 3600
graffiatodc.com / Open daily

Since I write about food and am always headed to the next new spot, there are few restaurants I visit repeatedly. Graffiato is one of them. The creation and personification of its masculine, tattooed chef and owner, Mike Isabella, Graffiato is all about creative comfort food. Pastas, vegetable plates and enormous pizzas are the name of the game. The gnocchi, served with ricotta and pork ragu, is the best I've sampled anywhere – including Florence. Arrive with an appetite and order two pies: the Countryman (black truffle, fontina and a soft farm egg), and the Jersey Shore, which comes topped with fried calamari rings and a cherry pepper aioli. Despite the industrial ambiance, Graffiato serves prosecco on tap – and I can certainly raise a glass to that.

MANDU

Seoul food

453 K Street NW (near 4 1/2 Street Street NW) / +1 202 289 6899
mandudc.com / Open daily

This might come as a shock, but there's more than fancy dining opportunities here. This city is rife with affordable and authentic eateries serving global dishes that often are overlooked. Enter Mandu, an unassuming, affordable Korean eating house on K Street. For the past decade, this family-run outfit has been serving generous helpings of its native cuisine alongside strong drinks. It's no wonder the place is always filled with foodies and chefs. You absolutely must order classics like the dumplings, bulgogi and kimchi — and be sure there's some marinated beef on your table. The weekend brunch is a spectacular deal: appetizers, an enormous platter of traditional Korean fare and mochi ice cream at a mere $15.

RASIKA

Sophisticated Indian fare

633 D Street NW (near 7th Street NW) / +1 202 637 1222
rasikarestaurant.com / Closed Sunday

Posh and contemporary, Rasika has long been a mainstay among politicians and upper-crust Washingtonians. To get a full experience, order the naan, the wildly popular (for very good reason) palak chaat, crispy spinach with yogurt, tamarind and date chutney, and at least one of the tandoori items — both the lamb and the chicken are amazing. A seafood lover, I was impressed with the rich shrimp malai, cooked with coconut milk and accented with mustard oil and bay leaves. It gets bonus points for being vegetarian-friendly and having a phenomenal wine list.

RED APRON BUTCHER

Nose-to-tail charcuterie

709 D Street NW (near 8th Street NW) / +1 202 524 5244
redapronbutchery.com / Open daily

A grab-and-go butcher, coffee and sandwich shop nestled in Penn Quarter, Red Apron Butchery is a collaboration between chef Nathan Anda and the Neighborhood Restaurant Group that features hormone- and antibiotic-free, sustainably raised beef, pork, lamb and poultry sourced from regional farmers. In addition to meats, there are more than 80 artisanal products, including crackers, jams and other accoutrements. What's more, there's a coffee bar — I've totally swung by here to pick up some prosciutto for my boyfriend and grabbed a caffeine boost for myself. We all have our vices.

WOOLLY MAMMOTH THEATRE

Award-winning, edgy live entertainment

641 D Street NW (near 7th Street NW) / +1 202 393 3939
woollymammoth.net / Open daily

Woolly Mammoth Theatre Company is conveniently located right
between Rasika (see page 51) and Oyamel, a Mexican dining concept from
José Andrés, the chef behind China Chilcano (see page 46), which makes
it the prime location for dinner and a show. This playhouse offers
high-quality, avant-garde shows at wallet-friendly prices. Serving as
a research and development unit for American theater, the productions
here are often groundbreaking and experimental. All the plays are daring,
thought-provoking and are definitely not for the modest – I've seen
nudity on their stage on no less than three separate occasions.

h street corridor

The gentrification of the H Street Corridor has been rapid. Though parts of it are still slightly dodgy, large swaths of H Street Northeast have become a veritable amusement park for adults. The strip that runs from 5th to 13th Streets has the most eclectic assortment of thematic venues I've ever seen: there's an Irish-Jewish bar, a sushi place that turns into a nightclub, a speakeasy disguised as a Chinese take-out joint, an Italian bistro with bocce ball courts and an Old English pub. And that's not even everything! You could spend many a Saturday night exploring the eccentric (and occasionally off-color) establishments – and trust me, I have – so here are my picks.

1 Biergarten Haus
2 DC Harvest (off map)
3 Granville Moore's
4 H Street Country Club
5 Maketto
6 Rock & Roll Hotel

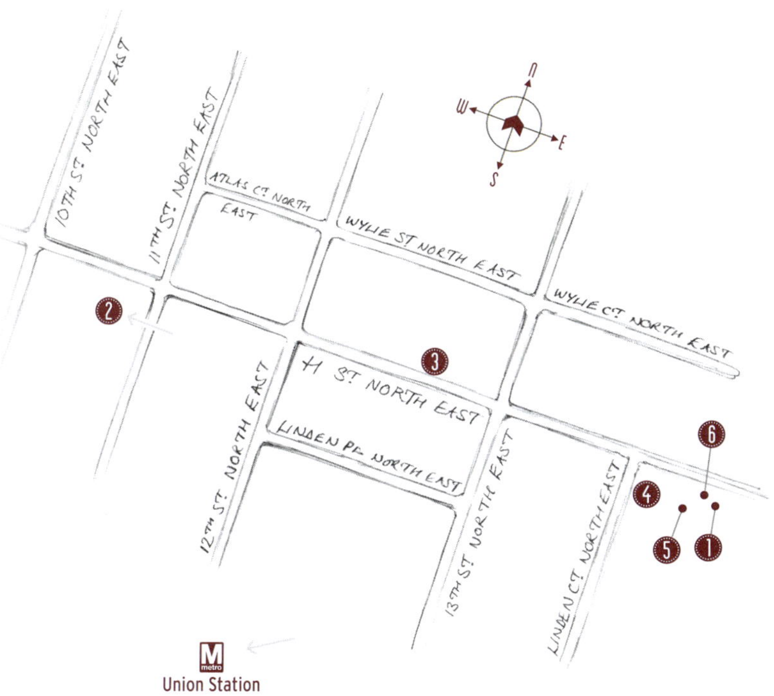

BIERGARTEN HAUS

A traditional German beer garden

1355 H Street NE (near Linden Court NE) / +1 202 388 4053
biergartenhaus.com / Open daily

As long as the air isn't frigid, D.C. residents love drinking outdoors.
This is perhaps because there are only a few al fresco places allowed in
the city due to zoning restrictions, which means that the local open-air
bars are usually busy. At Biergarten Haus, the amiable crowd packs the
communal picnic tables, downing Belgian brews out of enormous steins.
When I swing by here, my order is a large hefeweizen and a basket of soft
pretzels served with beer cheese and mustard to share with everyone
around me, whether I knew them before I arrived or not.

DC HARVEST

Farm-to-fork eats

517 H Street NE (near 6th Street NE) / +1 202 629 3296
dc-harvest.com / Open daily

With so many seasonal, New American dining concepts to choose from in one city, it can be hard to discern where to go. DC Harvest differentiates itself in that it sources 95% of its food from the Chesapeake Bay Watershed – no easy feat. The fruits and veggies served are only what's growing at the time, and the meats come from farms where livestock are grass-fed and humanely raised. What's more, unlike many of the small-plate spots in town, this one has hearty portions. The scallops and short ribs are my two recommendations for entrées. Obsessed with bacon? Swing by for the affordable brunch featuring house-cured rashers and bacon doughnuts.

GRANVILLE MOORE'S

Memorable grub at a hole-in-the-wall

1238 H Street NE (near 13th Street NE) / +1 202 399 2546
granvillemoores.com / Open daily

Without so much as a sign on the door, this Belgian brew pub named after a '50s-era D.C. doc has gained notoriety for its outstanding moules frites: the traditional white wine and garlic version is always satisfying, and the mussels with Hook's blue cheese is a showstopper. The fries are so tasty I once had a dream about them: they come twice-fried and served in an enormous bowl with a trio of housemade mayonnaises for dipping. (I feel confident declaring the truffle mayo as the best.) Wash down your meal with one of their 50-plus bottled beers, and you're all set.

H STREET COUNTRY CLUB

Indoor amusements and Tex-Mex

**1335 H Street NE (at Linden Court NE) / +1 202 399 4722
hstreetcountryclub.com / Open daily**

I love activities, and H Street Country Club is all about them. The name of the place might have you thinking it's all croquet and genteel card games, but the "country club" part is tongue-in-cheek — this dive bar is anything but. What it is, is a sure bet for a good time. The above-average pub eats are accompanied by skeeball, pool tables, darts and other bar game mainstays, and upstairs, there's an entire D.C.-themed mini golf course that includes King Kong climbing the Washington Monument. Bring your quarters, order up a margarita (skinny, if you must) on the rocks and chicken nachos, then settle in for a fun night out.

Asian street food, espresso and shoes

1351 H Street NE (near Linden Court NE) / +1 202 838 9972
maketto1351.com / Open daily

Maketto is a hipster's dream come true: a snazzy, selectively curated shop featuring sneakers, clothing and reading material with a hidden espresso bar and Cambodian-Taiwanese restaurant. The mixed-use venture with an inviting outdoor space is nouveau for the city, and attracts the artistic community. I'm more into their eats, and tend to drop by for the incredible Khmer nosh, and the easy-to-share plates make it one of my regulars for gatherings.

ROCK & ROLL HOTEL

Local live music

1353 H Street NE (near Linden Court NE) / +1 202 388 7625
rockandrollhoteldc.com / Closed Sunday

Rock & Roll Hotel is an appropriately gritty concert hall with three vastly different spaces. The concerts take place on the ground floor, on weekends there's always a DJ spinning up on level two and there's a chill rooftop bar that's perfect for a break from the noise or for meeting up with friends. The venue brings in bands from all along the East Coast, and, if rock is your thing, it's definitely worth taking a look at the lineup when you're in town. If White Ford Bronco, a fantastic '90s cover band, is playing, you must go; their shows are always a nostalgic blast.

meals on wheels

Gourmet food served from trucks

The District is filled with people who work hard on serious issues. At lunch every weekday, worker bees flock from their office buildings and government compounds to the nearest outdoor park, which will most likely be surrounded by food trucks. Though there are hundreds of roving kitchens here, only a few shine.

Falafel and fries are the name of the game at **DC Ballers**. The scrumptious Greek fries are topped with oregano, feta cheese and olive oil, and come with three dipping sauces. I didn't know the Greeks did French fries, but my stomach is happy that they do. Ravenous? Then the falafel platter is a smart buy, as it includes falafel balls, tabbouleh, a tomato and cucumber salad and garlic hummus with za'atar-dusted pita.

I was raised in Argentina, the land of the empanada, so when I discovered there was a food truck dedicated to my most favorite food, I was ecstatic but skeptical. I'm pleased to report **DC Empanadas** passes muster. The flavors vary weekly, but you can always count on both meat and vegetarian options being available. If the Ropanada, made with shredded beef and rice in a tomato base, or the Ménage à Trois, with brie, figs and Marcona almonds, are on the menu, order them.

Takorean, a bright blue and yellow truck, serves up Korean barbecue. Served in corn tortillas, these creative tacos come in flavors like bulgogi, soy and kimchi, and are available as pork, chicken, beef and tofu. Be sure to get the marinated pork shoulder with kale, purple cabbage and carrot tossed in a dressing of soy and gochugaro (hot red pepper flakes).

At **The Big Cheese**, you'll find grilled cheese sandwiches for grown-ups. My preference is the Mt. Fuji, with creamy, oozy Camembert, apples and honey, and I have many Tex-Mex-loving friends who swear by the Thrilled Cheese – chipotle cheddar, jalapeño and guacamole. The seasonal soups, like butternut squash and gazpacho, are also gratifying and fab for dipping.

Want something sweet? Hit up **Captain Cookie & The Milk Man** for – what else? – cookies and milk (skim, whole, chocolate or soy) or a chipwich (ice cream sandwich), which, for me, is the real draw. To order, choose a flavor of rich ice cream and two cookies (chocolate chip, vegan chocolate chip, snickerdoodle or Nutella) and these food truck saints will whip it up.

CAPTAIN COOKIE & THE MILK MAN

CAPTAIN COOKIE & THE MILK MAN
Visit website for daily locations, +1 202 556 3396
captaincookiedc.com

DC BALLERS
Visit @DcBallers on Twitter for daily locations
+1 202 340 1171, dcballer.com

DC EMPANADAS
Visit @DCEmpanadas on Twitter for daily locations
+1 703 400 5363, dcempanadas.com

TAKOREAN
Visit website for locations, no phone, takorean.com

THE BIG CHEESE
Visit website for daily locations, +1 703 855 6987
bigcheesetruck.com

capitol hill

With the US Capitol anchoring the neighborhood, it's no surprise that Capitol Hill is the heart of old Washington. It was originally composed of boarding houses for members of Congress; the Navy Yard, where ships were built and repaired; and the Marine Barracks, the location of which was selected by Thomas Jefferson during his presidency. Today, members of Congress make the move here (if only temporarily), taking up residence in the stately townhouses that line the streets, and congressional staffers keep the bars in business. But there's more here than politicians and government workers around. Though the area is largely residential, it does have its fair share of eateries and shops. The place really comes alive on weekends, when strolling through Eastern Market and Barracks Row are the name of the game. In fact, I'm often found here on a Saturday. I'll never tire of spending a day on Capitol Hill.

1 Barrel
2 Beuchert's Saloon
3 Capitol Hill Books
4 District Doughnut (off map)
5 Garrison
6 Hill's Kitchen
7 Labyrinth Games & Puzzles
8 Medium Rare
A ST. SOUTH EAST
INDEPENDENCE AVE. SOUTH EAST
NORTH CAROLINA AVE SOUTH EAST
C ST. SOUTH EAST
SEWARD SQ.
7TH ST. SOUTH EAST
8TH ST. SOUTH EAST
9TH ST. SOUTH EAST
5TH ST. SOUTH EAST
D ST. SOUTH EAST
M metro
Eastern Market
SOUTH CAROLINA AVE. SOUTH EAST
MARION PARK
E ST. SOUTH EAST
6TH ST. SOUTH EAST
G ST. SOUTH EAST

BARREL

A bar with stomach-hugging entrées

613 Pennsylvania Avenue SE (near 6th Street SE) / +1 202 543 3622
barreldc.com / Open daily

Sometimes I crave a homey, masculine watering hole, and Barrel is just that. It offers more than a hundred whiskeys, and lists the day's specials on gigantic chalkboards above the long, wooden bar. It's worth noting that this spot isn't just a place to knock back a few — it also has delish cuisine. Barrel's executive chef, Garret Fleming, makes most things — from the sausages to the noodles — from scratch. The food here is hearty, so you should come hungry and know that you'll leave full. At dinner, order one of the housemade pastas, and at brunch, don't miss the chicken and biscuits served with sausage gravy and delectable bourbon peach jam.

BEUCHERT'S SALOON

Storied pub

623 Pennsylvania Avenue SE (near 6th Street SE) / +1 202 733 1384
beuchertssaloon.com / Open daily

Capitol Hill is blessed. Right down the street from Barrel lies Beuchert's Saloon; with dim lighting and a subtle glamour, it always makes me want to linger. Above the marble, backlit bar is a hulking bison head, and at the back of the narrow space, the tables are often pushed together to accommodate groups. Beuchert's has quite the history – a tavern by the same name was founded in 1880, and during Prohibition, it operated as a speakeasy disguised as a Singer sewing machine store and then a gramophone shop. I recommend you make a reservation, and when you settle in for dinner, work your way through the charcuterie and cheese boards before ordering a burger and seasonal veggies. It goes without saying, but I'll say it anyway: you should also order a cocktail.

CAPITOL HILL BOOKS

Cheeky, whimsical bookshop

657 C Street SE (near 7th Street SE) / +1 202 544 1621
capitolhillbooks-dc.com / Open daily

I love Capitol Hill Books for two reasons: it's eccentric, and it's fun to peruse after a few mimosas. The long-standing store specializes in used and rare books, as well as first editions, and sits just around the corner from the line of bistros on 6th and Pennsylvania, so it's convenient to stop in after a meal. The snug, two-level shop is bursting with tomes – you'll find foreign language titles in the bathroom and cookbooks in the kitchen (naturally) – and is split into sections such as Mystery Room, Business Closet and Weird Section, which touts horror and paranormal titles. Visiting here is always an adventure!

DISTRICT DOUGHNUT

Sweet treats

749 8th Street SE (near I Street SE) / +1 202 750 1955
districtdoughnut.com / Closed Monday

On charming Barracks Row, located across from the Marine Barracks, lies a bright turquoise shop run by three enthusiastic Washingtonians. District Doughnut might look vibrant and playful, but they take their baking seriously and change their gourmet offerings weekly. The dulce de leche topped with sea salt is hands down the tastiest confection I've ever had and the chai crème brûlée is the best kind of decadence. Be sure to visit the darling bakery for hot-and-fresh deliciousness and a cup of coffee sourced from local roaster, Compass Coffee (see pg 33).

GARRISON

Inventive, ever-changing plates

524 8th Street SE (near G Street SE)
+1 202 506 2445 / garrisondc.com
Closed Monday

I imagine it's as hard for the many New American restaurants in the city to distinguish themselves from each other as it is for me to decide which I like most. At Garrison, there's a neutral white-and-wood design aesthetic that's beautiful, but doesn't take away from the real reason you're here: the food. The concept is farm-to-table, and the dishes pay homage to the bounty of nearby producers. Order a smattering of fresh vegetables and pasta made from scratch daily, and don't forget something from the raw menu, such as the absolutely spectacular bison tartare or the fluke crudo with lemon, fennel and horseradish, which is a sight to behold. The food is almost too pretty to eat — but when you dive in, you'll want to savor every bite.

HILL'S KITCHEN

Carefully selected culinary goods

713 D Street SE (near 8th Street SE) / +1 202 543 1997
hillskitchen.com / Closed Monday

My kitchen is the one place in my house where everything needs to be orderly or I get grumpy. When it's a mess, I feel like throwing everything out and going straight to Hill's Kitchen to start over. Entering the store and seeing essentials like oven mitts, crisp linen towels and mixing utensils, as well as whimsical cookie cutters in the shapes of the states that make up the country immediately banishes my little black cloud. What really brightens my mood is strolling through the store with owner Leah Daniels, who knows how to zero in on the most useful cooking tools.

LABYRINTH GAMES & PUZZLES

Hard-to-find tabletop entertainment

645 Pennsylvania Avenue SE (near 7th Street SE) / +1 202 544 1059
labyrinthgameshop.com / Closed Monday

Sorry, Milton Bradley, but Monopoly is so passé: mortgages and bankruptcies are suddenly not much fun anymore. For game night, we've moved on to specialty options, like the strategic Settlers of Catan and family-friendly, train-themed Ticket to Ride. Whatever you're into, be it role-playing, cards, classic jigsaw puzzles, brainteasers or chess, there's something for everyone at Labyrinth Games & Puzzles. This is a store that feels more like a community. When you visit, it's likely there will be groups playing cards inside the store, and the shop also hosts events and competitions around town. If it's been a while since you've shopped for a board game, you'll be surprised at what you've been missing.

MEDIUM RARE

A simple meal of steak and fries

515 8th Street SE (near E Street SE) / +1 202 601 7136
mediumrarerestaurant.com / Open daily

There's only one choice for dinner at Medium Rare — a $20 prix fixe of artisanal bread, a side salad and steak frites — and that's all you need. Inspired by L'Entrecote in Paris, the exposed brick interior, masterfully prepared bites and selectively curated wine and beer list combine to become my top choice for an affordable, relaxed date night. Save room in your tummy because there's little reason not to splurge on a slice of key lime pie or the enormous hot fudge sundae.

DOWNTOWN HOLIDAY MARKET
At 8th and F Streets NW (Penn Quarter)
downtownholidaymarket.com, +1 202 215 6993
open daily Thanksgiving to Christmas

DUPONT CIRCLE FRESHFARM MARKET
20th Street NW (near Massachusetts Avenue NW;
Dupont Circle), +1 202 362 8889
freshfarmmarkets.org, open Sundays

EASTERN MARKET
225 7th Street SE (near C Street SE; Capitol Hill)
+1 202 698 5253, easternmarket-dc.org
closed Monday

UNION MARKET
1309 5th Street NE (near Neal Place NE;
Northeast Washington), +1 301 347 3998
unionmarketdc.com, closed Monday

D.C. residents love to spend their weekends outdoors, and the plethora of markets in neighborhoods around the city provides a fantastic opportunity to do just that, especially on Saturday and Sunday mornings.

The original farmers market is **Dupont Circle FRESHFARM Market**, which is open on Sundays year-round. Head here to peruse fruits, vegetables and flowers from the Chesapeake Bay Watershed, and snag fresh loaves of bread or pick up a sandwich from a local vendor. I go for the empanadas and make sure to try all the cheeses and apples as I make my way around.

To get a real sense of the city's vibrant community, spend a weekend morning at **Eastern Market**, located in its namesake neighborhood off Capitol Hill. Inside you'll find smoothie vendors, butcher shops, bakeries, fishmongers and a breakfast counter with an inconceivably long line regardless of your arrival time.

The stalls outside are a mix of arts and crafts, and food stalls (you can't go wrong with the crêpes). Around the corner lies an antiques and vintage market, where I always shop for jewelry, records and furniture.

In the warehouse district of Northeast Washington, you'll find **Union Market**, a mixed-use development that contains more than 40 purveyors. Grab coffee at Peregrine and a bagel at Buffalo & Bergen, then continue to check out the market and taste all the freebies. When you need some fresh air, pop outside to visit the bar housed in an Airstream and to play cornhole on the lawn.

In D.C. near the end of the year? Be sure to hit up the **Downtown Holiday Market**. An ideal winter evening for me is ice skating at the National Gallery of Art's Sculpture Garden followed by a stroll through this market's aisles, purchasing artisanal gifts for me and mine.

georgetown

With its cobblestone streets and lovely houses trimmed with ivy, Georgetown is brimming with charm. Founded in 1751, the neighborhood actually predates the District of Columbia. Home to several embassies, Georgetown University and Old Stone House, the oldest unchanged residence in the city, this area is a must-visit for those who want colonial scenery while partaking in some serious retail therapy. Because of its historical appeal and fab shopping, it can be packed. I suggest avoiding the crowd on M Street and heading to the waterfront to enjoy the views of the Potomac River before hitting Dumbarton Oaks Park and Book Hill Park for a dose of nature. To add some new duds to your closet, stroll up Wisconsin Avenue, where you'll find boutiques aplenty, as well as scrumptious gelato.

VOLTA PL. NORTH WEST
2
6
9
P ST. NORTH WEST
O ST. NORTH WEST
O ST. NORTH WEST
DUMBARTON ST. NORTH WEST
WEST
WEST
NORTH
ST. NORTH
N ST. NORTH WEST
WISCONSIN AVE. NORTH WEST
PROSPECT ST. NORTH WEST
33RD ST.
POTOMAC
M ST. NORTH WEST
CADY'S ALLEY NW
7
8
10
CHESAPEAKE & OHIO CANAL TOWPATH
GRACE ST. NORTH WEST
31st ST. NORTH WEST
OLD STONE HOUSE PARK
30th ST. NORTH WEST
5
NORTH WEST
SOUTH ST. NORTH WEST
1
THOMAS JEFFERSON ST.
WHITEHURST FWY. NORTH WEST
GEORGETOWN WATERFRONT PARK
4
POTOMAC RIVER
3
1   Chez Billy Sud
2   Dolcezza (off map)
3   Fiola Mare
4   Georgetown Waterfront Park
5   Hu's Shoes and Hu's Wear
6   Lynn Louisa (off map)
7   Olivia Macaron
8   Relish
9   Sherman Pickey (off map)
10 Well Built

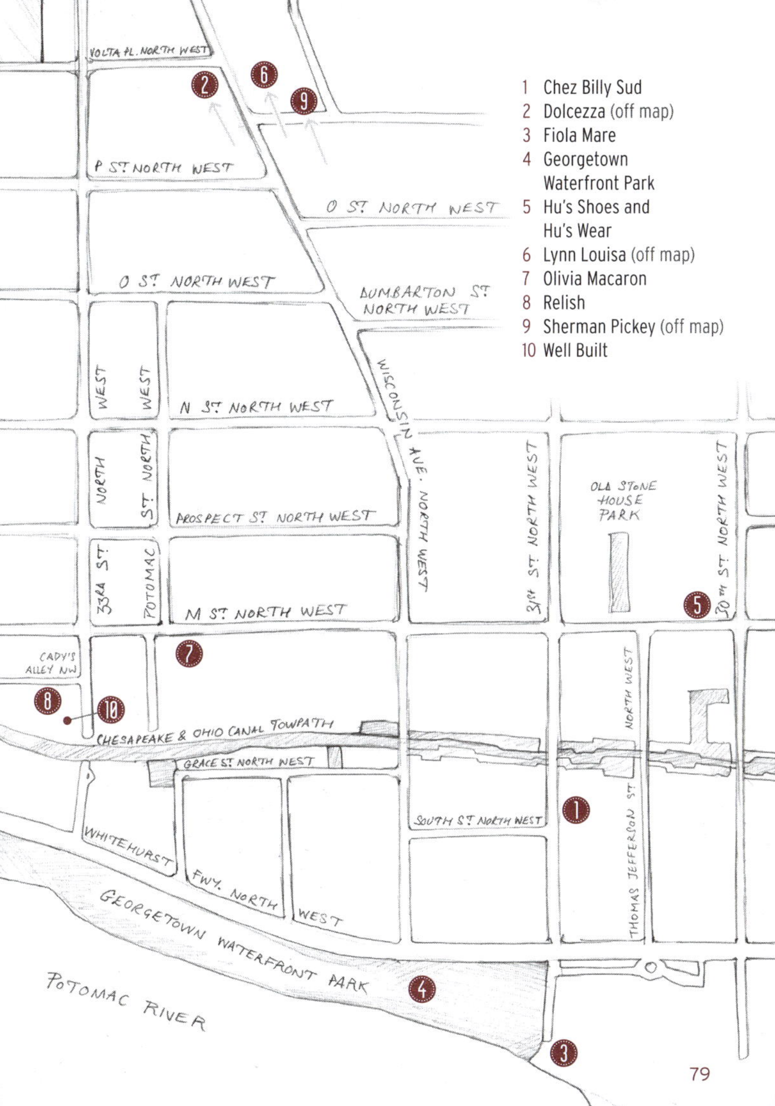

79

CHEZ BILLY SUD

An intimate space serving French fare

1039 31st Street NW (near South Street NW) / +1 202 965 2606
chezbillysud.com / Open daily

Nestled in a snug brick building with a bright blue door and sign, Chez Billy Sud oozes 19th-century southern French appeal with its antiquated light fixtures and paintings. The cuisine pairs seamlessly with the aesthetic: the bistro serves Provençal dishes and craft cocktails in vintage barware, of course. After a day of shopping or an event-filled week, I'll post up at the back bar with a girlfriend and order the so-simple-but-so-heavenly steak frites and a glass of red wine. The restaurant's other classics, particularly the beef bourguignon and the sautéed trout with capers and brown butter sauce, are also *magnifique*.

DOLCEZZA

Icy artisanal delights

1560 Wisconsin Ave NW (at Q Street NW) / **+1 202 333 0933**
dolcezzagelato.com / **Open daily**

The love story behind the creation of Dolcezza is one of South American romance and gelato – so basically the best story. Owner Robb was traveling through South America when he met and fell in love with Violeta, who hails from Argentina. They visited a popular gelataria in Buenos Aires, and it was there that the idea to bring the Argentine-style treat to the United States was born. Having been raised in Buenos Aires myself, I'm grateful to be able to find Argentine gelato – which is thicker, smoother and richer than the Italian version – whenever I get a craving (which is often!). By combining fruits and herbs from local markets, Robb turns seasonal goodness into frozen magic with flavors ranging from salted caramel to pink grapefruit to orange honey cardamom.

FIOLA MARE

High-end dining

**3050 K Street NW, Suite 101 (near 31st Street NW) / +1 202 628 0065
fiolamaredc.com / Open daily**

Fiola Mare is my preferred location for special occasions, even if the occasion is merely that I'd like to go there. The waterfront space is luxurious, with high ceilings, mahogany flooring, banquet booths upholstered with plush, striped fabric and floor-to-ceiling windows. The vibe is nautical yet glam – almost as if you're having dinner on a yacht. There's also a magnificent raw bar, and you can see the catch of the day sitting on ice in front of the open kitchen. It's no surprise, then, that I recommend you order a seafood meal, and remember to save room for dessert: there are delectable ricotta doughnuts to be had.

GEORGETOWN WATERFRONT PARK

Gather by the river

Water Street NW (along Capitol Crescent Trail) / **No phone**
georgetownwaterfrontpark.org / **Open daily**

One of my routine outdoor weekend activities is strolling down the hill to Georgetown Waterfront Park. The clean green space is anchored by an enormous fountain, where children often splash around, and it's the start of several running paths that lead both toward the city, as well as into the wooded Chesapeake & Ohio Canal National Historic Park. I usually make my way down to the granite, stadium-style steps at the edge of the river, a sublime locale for sitting and chatting while watching the boaters and birds on the Potomac as planes from Reagan Airport fly in and out overhead. On more adventurous summer days, I'll head around the corner to Jack's Boat House to rent paddleboards or kayaks with friends.

HU'S SHOES AND HU'S WEAR

Fine clothing and footwear

Hu's Shoes: 3005 M Street NW (near 30th Street NW)
+ 1 202 342 0202 / hushoes.com / Open daily

Hu's Wear: 2906 M Street NW (near 29th Street NW)
+1 202 342 2020 / husonline.com / Open daily

Located at the start of M Street and situated a block apart, Hu's Shoes and Hu's Wear are the original luxury boutiques in Georgetown. The range of designer ready-to-wear clothing is the closest you'll get to Fashion Week in Washington – the owner heads to Manhattan, Paris and Milan to shop the lines each season, sourcing creative and bold pieces. The bags are divine, with the latest from Chloé, Valentino, Fendi and more off-the-cuff brands like Eddie Borgo. Plus, over at Hu's Shoes, you'll find designs from Jimmy Choo, Chie Mihara and Officine Creative. It's no wonder that these shops have been in business for nearly a decade and are touted regularly by Washingtonian elites as well as publications like *Travel & Leisure* and Refinery 29. Now, if only I could afford that Chloé bag I've been eyeing.

LYNN LOUISA

Under-the-radar women's brands

1631 Wisconsin Avenue NW (near Q Street NW) / +1 202 350 0406
lynnlouisa.com / Open daily, Mondays by appointment

In an appealing white cottage on Wisconsin Avenue lies Lynn Louisa,
one of Georgetown's few remaining independently owned womenswear
boutiques. And thank goodness, as I regularly drop by the shop when
I'm in need of something stylish and unique. Brands include US-based
DREW, and Scandinavian labels Samsøe & Samsøe and Just Females. The
selections are high quality, chic and elegant, making the shop a fabulous
place to invest in a silk blouse or cashmere sweater you'll keep in your
closet for years to come.

OLIVIA MACARON

Flavorful pastry specialist

3222 M Street NW (near Potomac Street NW) / +1 202 965 1000
oliviamacaron.com / Open daily

Many weary Georgetown shoppers will brave the seemingly never-ending line at Georgetown Cupcake, or turn the corner defeated and head to Dean & Deluca for an afternoon treat. I do neither, choosing instead to hop to Olivia Macaron for a pick-me-up. The cheerful patisserie serves only the delicate meringue confections and coffee, and you won't find me complaining. The French macarons here are as good, if not better, than the big-named Parisian chains. Though it's hard to choose, the salted caramel is my constant, but I also like to try the fun flavors like Fruity Pebbles, gingerbread and matcha (another personal favorite). The best part? They're made with almond flour, so this treat is gluten-free, which is one of the many reasons I'll devour a whole box of them by myself.

RELISH

A well-stocked shop for the well-heeled

**3312 Cady's Alley NW (near 33rd Street NW) / +1 202 333 5343
relishdc.com / Closed Sunday**

Found off M Street and down the stairs in Cady's Alley, Relish is a serene, two-level boutique with high ceilings, wooden floors and pristine displays of haute fashion pieces. Owner Nancy Pearlstein understands sartorial fantasy, and her store's vision acknowledges runway lust. The brands carried here are pret-a-porter lines you won't find elsewhere in Washington — or many other places for that matter. The list of designers stocked at the shop reads like a fashion porn novel: think Simone Rocha, Dries Van Noten and Gary Graham. Even if you can't afford a thing, it's worth a visit for the joy of perusal alone. Relish is serious retail seduction.

SHERMAN PICKEY

Preppy fashions in a charming cottage

1647 Wisconsin Avenue NW (near Reservoir Road NW)
+1 202 333 4212 / shermanpickey.com / Closed Monday

The shopping at Sherman Pickey is worth a sweaty stroll up the hill that is Wisconsin Avenue. This store is the epitome of the classic, collegiate style that's made Georgetown famous. The bright yellow row house is filled with American-made wares for men and women, from small brands like Ledbury, Southern Tide, Sail to Sable and Elizabeth McKay to larger namesakes like Tory Burch, Kate Spade and Saint James. Be sure to don your new duds down the street at Martin's Tavern – where JFK proposed to Jackie – for boozing and schmoozing with the prepsters.

WELL BUILT

Beautiful, eco-friendly furniture

**1028 33rd Street NW, #320 (near Cady's Alley NW) / +1 202 299 0597
wellbuiltllc.com / By appointment only**

Sustainability is a buzzword of our time, and Ann Blackwell, owner of Well Built, has a philosophy: responsible design is responsible living. Her boutique only carries brands that meet her very high standards. When she reviews a new line, she asks three questions: How much energy goes into producing it? How long will it last? Does it contain no- or low-volatile organics? With such thoughtful vetting, she has curated a gorgeous collection featuring lines like De La Espada and Misewell. Well Built also sources green products from independent brands and small designers that share the same vision. I love perusing the artistic pieces, as it's easy to see the craft and care put into each one, from the creation to the curation.

fresh air

Greener pastures

One of the things that first drew me to Washington was the access to running trails, outdoor parks and weekend excursions. The District lies in close proximity to a bevy of nature reserves, and boasts more outdoor paths than any city in the nation. Though you can visit vineyards, parks and horse farms in the surrounding areas of Virginia and Maryland, you can take in Mother Nature right here in one of the dozens of green spaces.

In the summer months, the US capital's parks, gardens and en plein air museums are filled with opportunities for stunning vistas, picnics, al fresco concerts and activities to get out and enjoy. The **National Gallery of Art Sculpture Garden** hosts its Jazz in the Garden on Friday evenings, when the park brims with groups lounging on blankets, noshing charcuterie and sipping sangria.

Other great picnicking sites can be found in Georgetown, which is rife with historic mansions. Located at the neighborhood's highest point, **Dumbarton Oaks** is a 53-acre estate with a historic home-turned-museum and breathtaking gardens that include terraces, benches, urns and fountains. As I've seen the museum before, I usually head straight to the gardens to enjoy an evening picnic and outdoor theater performance.

Hillwood Estate, Museum and Gardens lies north, near family-friendly Forest Hills. Once owned by Marjorie Merriweather Post, the museum showcases the alluring collection of Russian Imperial art, Fabergé eggs and French decorative pieces she amassed during her lifetime. Be sure to stop by the museum even if the weather doesn't hold out for you to see the gardens.

Across town, there's the **United States National Arboretum**, which, in addition to collections of dogwoods, ferns, magnolias and firs, is also home to stunning bonsai gardens and beautiful columns formerly from the US Capitol that are perfect for Instagram shots.

If you visit the National Mall, factor in time for a trip to **Tidal Basin**, a reservoir situated between the Potomac River and Washington Channel. You'll see the impressive Jefferson Memorial across the water, which is especially awe-inspiring during the Cherry Blossom Festival held each spring. The trek around the whole basin is worth your while – as are stops at the Franklin Delano Roosevelt and Martin Luther King, Jr. Memorials.

DUMBARTON OAKS

3120 R Street NW (near 32nd Street NW; Georgetown)
+1 202 339 6480, doaks.org, closed Monday

HILLWOOD ESTATE, MUSEUM AND GARDENS

4155 Linnean Avenue NW (near Broad Branch Road NW;
near Forest Hills), +1 202 686 5807
hillwoodmuseum.org, closed Monday

NATIONAL GALLERY OF ART SCULPTURE GARDEN

Between Constitution Avenue and Madison Drive
(near 7th Street; near Penn Quarter), +1 202 737 4215
nga.gov/content/ngaweb/visit/maps-and-information/
sculpture-garden.html, open daily

TIDAL BASIN

West Basin Drive SW (near Independence Avenue SW;
near National Mall), +1 800 628 7275, no website
open daily

UNITED STATES NATIONAL ARBORETUM

3501 New York Avenue SE (near Hickey Lane NE;
Northeast Washington), +1 202 245 2726
usna.usda.gov, open daily

UNITED STATES NATIONAL ARBORETUM

dupont circle

Arguably the most recognizable neighborhood in Washington, D.C., posh Dupont Circle is located in the middle of the city and demarcated by its namesake roundabout. Built in the 1800s by architect Pierre Charles L'Enfant, the area is known for its attractive brownstones, as well as the jaw-dropping Embassy Row that lines Massachusetts Avenue. Aside from fantastic architecture, there are also dozens of bars, casual lunch spots and restaurants. On weekends, the circle is filled with all sorts of activities: duos playing chess, groups of beatboxers and dancers entertaining crowds, free yoga classes and running group meet-ups. I often head to this hood for a workout class and take my time making my way home, always stopping at the Dupont Circle Fountain with a friend to people-watch.

S ST NORTH WEST
RIGGS PL. NORTH WEST
R ST. NORTH WEST
CORCORAN ST. NORTH WEST
CONNECTICUT AVE.
NORTH WEST
AVE. NORTH WEST
Q ST. NORTH WEST
M metro
Dupont Circle Metro Station
NEW HAMPSHIRE
CHURCH ST. NORTH WEST
P ST. NORTH WEST
DUPONT CIRCLE NORTH WEST
NORTH WEST
HOPKINS ST.
NORTH WEST
O ST. NORTH WEST
MASSACHUSETTS AVE. NORTH WEST
SUNDERLAND PL.
NORTH WEST
18TH ST. NORTH WEST
20TH ST. NORTH WEST
19TH ST. NORTH WEST
N ST. NORTH WEST
RHODE ISLAND AVE. NORTH WEST
1   DGS Delicatessen
2   Glen's Garden Market
3   Hudson & Crane (off map)
4   Iron Gate
5   Kramerbooks & Afterwords
6   Little Serow (off map)
7   Proper Topper

DGS DELICATESSEN

Reinvented lunch counter

1317 Connecticut Ave NW (near N Street NW) / +1 202 293 4400
dgsdelicatessen.com / Open daily

Owned by two cousins, DGS Delicatessen uses traditional brining, curing, smoking and pickling techniques for its meat, fish and vegetables. The name is a nod to the District Grocery Stores cooperative that was popular in the early- and mid-1900s, and were often run by Jewish families; but with white subway tiles and high ceilings, the space is a modernized version of the stores of yore. Drop in for an appetizing meal of authentic Jewish staples: house-cured pastrami, duck fat matzo balls and bagels and lox. Hit up the cozy bar tucked in the back for excellent mixed drinks, like the cheekily named Mazel Tov Cocktail, consisting of rosé prosecco, gin, lavender syrup and lemon.

GLEN'S GARDEN MARKET

All-local grocer

2001 S Street NW (at 20th Street NW) / +1 202 588 5698
glensgardenmarket.com / Open daily

If you truly want to experience Washington's food and people, then a visit to Glen's Garden Market is an absolute must. The women-led store sources only products from the Chesapeake Bay Watershed, which means you won't be finding any pineapples in the produce section. What you will find are meats, cheeses, fruits, veggies and wines that are all top notch and enticingly fresh. Beyond the grocery, Glen's has a pizza and sandwich bar and an enormous, pet-friendly outdoor patio where you can enjoy the area's beers and vinos. Fair warning, it fills up quickly during lunch and happy hour. Glen's is the heart of the Dupont Circle and small business community, so definitely stop by, and tell them I said hello.

HUDSON & CRANE

Unique housewares and gifts

**1781 Florida Avenue NW (near California Street NW) / +1 202 436 1223
hudsonandcrane.com / Closed Monday**

This urban mercantile is filled to the brim with handpicked furniture, funky accessories and coffee table books. The large pieces, like sofas, dressers and rugs, tend to be mid-century or vintage-inspired. There are plenty of affordable home accessories like pillows, poufs and assorted details that will lend a distinctive touch to your casa and fit in your suitcase. Personally, I have a thing for throw pillows and candles, and I've added several to my stock from Hudson & Crane.

IRON GATE

Washington's oldest place for a meal

1734 N Street NW (near 17th Street NW) / +1 202 524 5202
irongaterestaurantdc.com / Open daily

With a carriage house established by General Miles during the Civil War
that later served as an inn, Iron Gate is a true dining relic. The narrow
space featuring the original brick walls now operates as a year-round bar
and restaurant, but the real reason to visit is the picturesque courtyard,
strung with wisteria and grape leaves. The Mediterranean dishes include
root vegetable panzanella, spanakopita and farro salad, and are served
family style or as shared plates. The wine list is expansive, and the
menu for the courtyard features bites like olives, kale salad, charcuterie,
burrata and more, all terrific for a midday or early evening snack.

KRAMERBOOKS & AFTERWORDS

Late-night reads and nosh

1517 Connecticut Avenue NW (near Q Street NW) / +1 202 387 1400
kramers.com / Open daily

Kramerbooks, a multi-concept bookshop that includes Afterwords, a café with a liquor license, is an institution here. The store is organized by topic – with hefty philosophy, politics and travel sections. I can always count on the staff picks, and I love that they build up local authors by displaying their titles in the window. Browsing the shelves solo? Keep in mind that this is a notorious pick-up spot, filled with eager singles chatting up potential dates based on their preferred choice of literature. If you're up past midnight, it's a fab place for a slice of housemade key lime pie or red velvet cake and a drink in the bar, which is open until 1am on weekdays and 3am on weekends. During the day, snag a seat in the bright atrium for a hearty and reliably tasty meal.

LITTLE SEROW

Thai food that's worth the wait

**1511 17th Street NW (near P Street NW) / No phone / littleserow.com
Closed Sunday and Monday**

A teeny tiny dining establishment, Little Serow serves up family style Isaan cuisine from northeastern Thailand, where owners Johnny Monis and Anne Marler honeymooned. You should note that this place has serious rules – no reservations! no photography! – and, usually, a long wait. The $49 prix fixe varies week to week, and if you order it, know that there are no substitutions or considerations on dietary restrictions (more rules!). If you can comply, then you're in for a treat. In my opinion, the first two courses of fresh Thai vegetables and noodle, no matter what they may be, are worth the visit – and that's before you're served the unbelievable pork ribs.

PROPER TOPPPER

Hats and gifts galore

1350 Connecticut Avenue NW (near Dupont Circle NW)
+1 202 842 3055 / propertopper.com / Open daily

I attend an annual garden party, and the dress code requires a sundress and fabulous headpiece. The frock is easy to handle, and since finding Proper Topper, the hat portion is, too. As the name implies, this is a shop dedicated to headwear, and it carries all styles, from floppy winter beanies to structured fedoras, whimsical fascinators to bejeweled headbands, and vintage bowlers to wide-brimmed sun hats. Beyond chapeaus, the Dupont Circle boutique carries an assortment of home goods and clothing, including thoughtful notecards, coffee table books and cute cotton dresses from brands like Paper Crown and Tracy Reese.

D.C. AFTER DARK:
modern speakeasies

Classic tipples, if you can find them

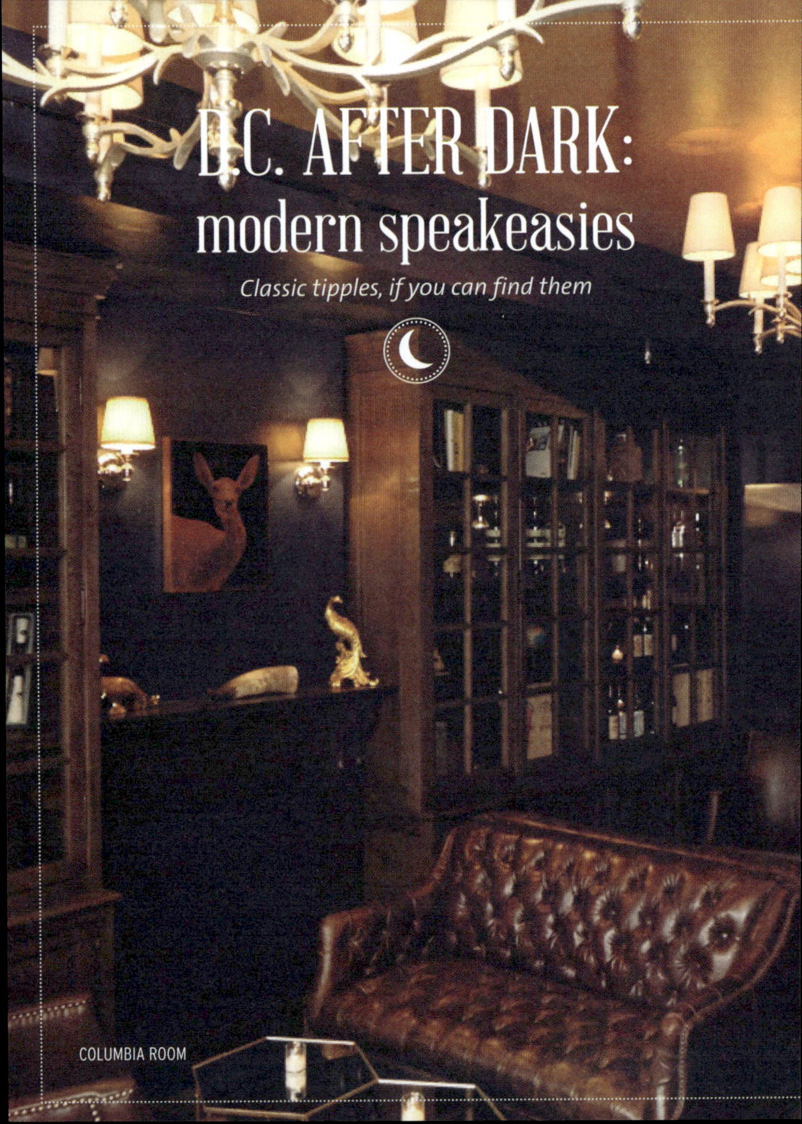

COLUMBIA ROOM
124 Blagden Alley NW (near 10th Street NW; Shaw)
+1 202 316 9398, columbiaroomdc.com
closed Monday

HAROLD BLACK
212 7th Street SE (near North Caroline Avenue SE;
Capitol Hill), +1 202 627 0994, haroldblackdc.com
closed Sunday and Monday

IVY AND CONEY
1537 7th Street NW (near Q Street NW; Shaw)
+1 202 670 9489, ivyandconey.com, open daily

THE GIBSON
2009 14th Street NW (near U Street NW;
U Street Corridor), +1 202 232 2156
thegibsondc.com, open daily

Washington has a number of hideaways dedicated to the art of the cocktail, in rather varied aesthetics and neighborhoods.

The Gibson, the District's first and premier secret drinking destination, transports you so thoroughly back to the 1920s that you'd swear you stepped into a time machine, if it weren't for the fact that it's modern hipsters behind the bar. This is certainly a place for the adventurous imbiber, as it serves up a huge list of refined drinks with kicky names, like the Frank Underwood (Malört, apple brandy, Kümmel, Campari and lemon) and the I Been Drankin' (Laphroaig 10, Midori, lime and raspberry).

Harold Black might be small in size and in menu, but it's a great place to stop after dinner on Capitol Hill. I dig the Lost in Translation, which includes bourbon and bitter grapefruit liqueur, but if bubbly is more your speed, the Cocktail #4 will do you nicely – chamomile and pear-infused vodka with apricot liqueur, lime and Champagne.

Want to be at D.C.'s "it" spot? May I present **Columbia Room** – the brainchild of Washington's famed mixologist Derek Brown – in Shaw's Blagden Alley. Here, you can choose your experience based on where you'd like to sit. On the charming rooftop patio is a punch garden serving booze in elegant coupes; inside, lies the spirits library, where you can repose in a leather armchair among mahogany bookshelves with an Omar Khayyám, made with bourbon, mulled orange wine and black lemon bitters, or The Last Cup, mixed with Pimms #1, Yellow Chartreuse, maraschino liqueur and verbena. For a more educational night, book a seat in the tasting room, which provides an intimate, five-course libation menu, including food pairings. The offerings rotate seasonally, and sure are memorable.

For those wanting something more casual, belly up at **Ivy & Coney**. The hidden sports-loving dive – though similar to speakeasies in that it's not easy to find unless you're in the know – eschews fancy drinks and pomp and circumstance, opting instead for cold beers and straight-up shots, peanuts (the shells of which end on the floor) and its famous hot dogs (all the better to soak up the liquor).

Whatever your preference, this city's got you covered. Bottoms up!

D.C. AFTER DARK:
live jazz & blues joints

For cool cats

The music scene in D.C. is a robust one with a long history. The historically African-American U Street Corridor was once known as the black Broadway (a phrase coined by the late African-American actress and singer Pearl Bailey) due to the prevalence of incredible musicians who performed nightly. These days, you can find live tunes all across the city, but these four are your best bets for a fantastic, groovy time.

Twins Jazz began in 1986 as an Ethiopian restaurant that served up a side of jazz. It now hosts two shows every Wednesday through Sunday, beginning at 9pm and 11pm, respectively. Tickets start at an affordable $10, and can be purchased either at the door or online. The music here is spectacular and the ambiance is casual – it's a no-fuss place for a stiff drink, delicious food and a marvelous night.

Around the corner lies **JoJo Restaurant and Bar**, a personal favorite given my penchant for Michael Jackson covers and upbeat vibes. The bands, encompassing every variety of jazz from New Orleans-style to Brazilian and Latin, are always entertaining, and the crowd is always friendly – this is definitely the type of venue where people dance in their seats. There's live music Tuesday through Sunday nights, and often a Sunday brunch concert as well.

For a rowdier experience, **New Vegas Lounge** is where it's at. There's epic live blues, and it's a go-to for people looking to take shots and snag a partner on the dance floor. If you love shaking it to the sounds of Marvin Gaye and Smokey Robinson, this is for you, but if you can't handle sweaty, noisy crowds of dancers, it's not. Do note that it's only open on Fridays and Saturdays – the band starts up at 10pm, and don't forget to bring $10 cash for the cover charge.

Across town is **Blues Alley**, the oldest jazz supper club in the nation, and a Georgetown institution. As you might expect, this place is a bit more upscale than its U Street counterparts: there's a reasonable per person food and beverage minimum, and a suggested business casual dress code. Blues Alley also defines itself as a "listening club," meaning conversations should be kept to a minimum during performances. Even so, it's terrific for hearing world-class musicians and having a sophisticated night on the town.

BLUES ALLEY
1073 Wisconsin Avenue NW (near M Street NW;
Georgetown), +1 202 337 4141, bluesalley.com
open daily

JOJO RESTAURANT AND BAR
1518 U Street NW (near 15th Street NW;
U Street Corridor), +1 202 319 9350, jojodc.com
closed Monday

NEW VEGAS LOUNGE
1415 P Street NW (near 14th Street NW;
Logan Circle), +1 202 483 3971, newvegasloungedc.com
open Friday and Saturday

TWINS JAZZ
1344 U Street NW (near 14th Street NW;
U Street Corridor), +1 202 234 0072, twinsjazz.com
open daily

BLUES ALLEY JAZZ

u street corridor

Just a few years back, the U Street Corridor was surviving on memories of its heyday as an early 20th-century center of black culture. Back then, it was the especially vibrant stomping ground of jazz genius Duke Ellington, poets Langston Hughes and Georgia Douglas Johnson, and musicians Louis Armstrong, Cab Calloway and Sarah Vaughan. In the 1950s, Thurgood Marshall organized the landmark *Brown v. Board of Education* case at the 12th Street YMCA. Then, in 1968, this was the epicenter of the destructive riots that erupted when news of Dr Martin Luther King, Jr.'s assassination broke. After that, many businesses and residents left the area, and it lost its luster. Thanks to a concentrated redevelopment effort, this diverse neighborhood has experienced a lively resurgence of culture, nightlife and renovation of many landmark buildings. Now, Ethiopian food, offbeat boutiques and live music are fueling the revival of the U Street Corridor.

1 DC Noodles
2 El Rey (off map)
3 Good Wood
4 Junction
5 Legendary Beast
6 Marvin
7 Satellite Room (off map)

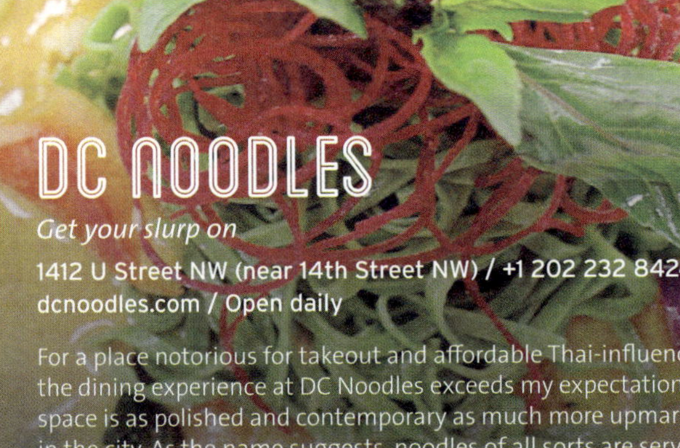

DC NOODLES

Get your slurp on

1412 U Street NW (near 14th Street NW) / +1 202 232 8424
dcnoodles.com / Open daily

For a place notorious for takeout and affordable Thai-influenced fare, the dining experience at DC Noodles exceeds my expectations. The small space is as polished and contemporary as much more upmarket places in the city. As the name suggests, noodles of all sorts are served up: wok-fried crowd-pleasers like pad Thai and pad see ew; curried options like Burmese kao soi, flavored with turmeric and cumin, and a green curry served with squid ink spaghetti; made-to-order noodle soups and salads, and that's only a few offerings. I'm confident you get the picture. Start your meal with edamame, Thai BBQ pork skewers and the exquisite dumplings (chicken and shrimp or seafood), and then order whichever dish catches your fancy.

EL REY

Tex-Mex in an unexpected environment

919 U Street NW (near Vermont Avenue NW) / +1 202 506 6418
elreydc.com / Open daily

It's hard to miss El Rey, as the Latin American taqueria and beer garden is built out of primary colored shipping containers. The interior is as playful as the exterior, with bright piñatas hanging from the banisters of the retractable roof (perfect for spring and summer brunches). The offerings here won't surprise you: it's all moreish tacos, tamales, tequila and cervezas. When I'm craving Mexican food with a Texas kick, El Rey is my preferred place to while away an afternoon or evening with good friends, enormous margaritas and baskets of chips and salsa.

RECOMMENDED BY **JANNA DOTSCHKAL**

ASSOCIATE PHOTO EDITOR AT NATIONAL GEOGRAPHIC

GOOD WOOD

American mercantile

1428 U Street NW (near Waverly Place NW)
+1 202 986 3640 / goodwooddc.com
Open daily

There are two boutiques I frequent weekly: Salt & Sundry (see pg 22) and Good Wood. Both carry home goods, barware and assorted gifts and accessories that never fail to inspire and delight. You might say I have a type, but I'm more than okay with it. What makes Good Wood different from Salt & Sundry, though, is that it's been in operation for more than 20 years, and is an enormous space filled with well-curated, affordable vintage furniture. Scattered throughout the shop is a selection of other items, including all-natural soaps and candles, a lovely assemblage of women's clothing and jewelry from under-the-radar brands and even the occasional handbag. Once you go, you'll be as hooked as I am.

JUNCTION

Retro duds for men and women

1510 U Street NW (near 15th Street NW) / +1 202 483 0261
junctionwdc.com / Closed Monday and Tuesday

Junction has been holding it down on U Street for more than a decade, and carries pre-loved clothing from the 1930s to today, with a heavy emphasis on '60s, '70s and '80s attire — think track jackets, cowboy boots, multi-colored caftans and evening gowns. The last time I visited, I was pleasantly surprised to see that the range of shoes and threads for gents was robust, as I've found that most shops specializing in secondhand apparel tend to focus on goods for the ladies. Another significant point about Junction is that new items are stocked regularly, which means I never get bored of browsing, even if I stop by once a week.

LEGENDARY BEAST

Hand-selected and economical baubles

1520 U Street NW (near 15th Street NW) / +1 202 797 1234
legendarybeast.com / Open Saturday and Sunday

Though much of U and 14th Streets are filled with antiques shops and boutiques hawking vintage clothing and accessories, only a few hold up when it comes to quality and affordability, especially in the realm of accessories. One store I can always count on when it comes to killer costume jewelry is Legendary Beast. Perched on the third floor of a row house, this treasure trove filled with bling is only open on weekends, so be sure to plan accordingly, especially if you have an event that requires a certain glitz or specific Art Deco-style necklace in the middle of the week.

MARVIN

Bringing a whole new meaning to "Let's Get It On"

2007 14th Street NW (near U Street NW) / +1 202 797 7171
marvindc.com / Open daily

A U Street institution, this outfit is a restaurant and rooftop bar dedicated to singer Marvin Gaye, who spent time in both D.C. and Belgium. I actually had my very first dinner out on the town here, and I've been bringing friends and visitors back to the sophisticated-yet-casual establishment ever since. The menu includes well-executed takes on Belgian and Southern classics like moules frites, fried chicken and waffles, shrimp and grits and an absolutely delicious burger topped with farmhouse cheddar, bacon, onion jam, and, if you so choose, a fried egg. When it comes to sweets, the warm toffee cake is heavenly. After your meal, make your way up to the roof to enjoy the views and chill with the locals.

SATELLITE ROOM

Boozy milkshakes

2047 9th Street NW (near V Street NW) / +1 202 506 2496
satellitedc.com / Open daily

Dark and edgy, this diner serves alcoholic shakes, burgers and beer
at all hours of the day and night – a necessity given its proximity to
9:30 Club, the busy concert venue. I love the décor here: the enormous
bar is backlit with an eponymous sign, there's Warhol-inspired artwork
on the cool, patterned tile walls and purple diner booths. But let's talk
about the milkshakes. I keep it simple, ordering the Vincent Vega,
a vanilla and bourbon concoction. However, there are funkier flavors:
espresso and Hennessy, avocado and tequila or peanut butter with
Tennessee whiskey. Come the weekend, Satellite Room's brunch offers
free-flow mimosas and Southern food – think chicken and biscuits
and thick stacks of pancakes.

columbia heights

Most Washingtonians head up the hill to wonderfully diverse Columbia Heights to visit Target and Bed Bath & Beyond – convenient, one-stop shopping chains that can't be found downtown. I prefer to come here for a low-key night out at one (or more) of the fantastic holes-in-the-wall and dive bars this neighborhood boasts. If you're looking for a more boisterous night on the town, The Wonderland Ballroom is just the ticket; it's a fun place to let loose and dance the night away even if the crowd does skew a bit young and hipster these days. Due to the very international mix of residents in this area, Columbia Heights is also known for its authentic global flavors, particularly its Vietnamese, Salvadoran and Mexican eats.

1 El Chucho
2 Kangaroo Boxing Club
3 Maple
4 RedRocks Neapolitan Bistro
5 Room 11
6 Thip Khao

OAK ST. NORTH WEST
MERIDIAN PL. NORTH WEST
NEWTON ST. NORTH WEST
NORTH WEST
MONROE ST.
PARK RD. NORTH
WEST
WEST
NORTH
14TH ST.
KENYON ST. NORTH WEST
LAMONT ST. NORTH WEST
10TH ST. NORTH WEST
11TH ST.
NORTH WEST
13TH ST.
NORTH WEST
IRVING ST. NORTH WEST
M metro
Columbia Heights

EL CHUCHO

A bright and festive Mexican joint

3313 11th Street NW (near Lamont Street NW) / +1 202 290 3313
elchuchodc.com / Open daily

It's all about tacos and tequila at El Chucho, which is easy to find with
its turquoise exterior and black-and-yellow sign. The laid-back eating house
has a splendid roof deck, stays open late and tends to be crowded no matter
when you turn up. Don't let that deter you, though. The prices are cheap,
but the portions are small: if you have a big appetite, you will probably need
two orders to feel fully sated. My usual is the savory pork tacos al pastor
and a margarita, of which there are many flavors, including spicy habanero.
You'll also find lots of imported Mexican brews, craft beers, wines and boozy
beverages with naughty names, like the Señor Clusterf*$k (a mix of whiskey,
mezcal and vermouth) if that's more your speed.

KANGAROO BOXING CLUB

House-smoked meats with a side of sports

3410 11th Street NW (near Park Road NW) / **+1 202 505 4522**
kangaroodc.com / **Open daily**

Kangaroo Boxing Club is owned by a bunch of dudes who cook for and cater to those who share their penchant for eating while watching a ball game. The mouthwatering dishes include pulled pork, ribs, pastrami, duck breast, brisket and wings, all smoked in-house. My boyfriend and I tend to come for rib night (Tuesdays and Fridays), when you can get slow-smoked St. Louis pork ribs with two sides for less than $20. When it comes to sides, I go for the mac and cheese, the fried Brussels sprouts and the Johnny Cakes – mini corn breads served with honey maple butter. Moreover, the wife of one of the owners is a vegetarian, so there's a surprising amount of meat-free items, like the falafel wrap, made with spinach, tzatziki, feta, lettuce and pickled veggies. Everything is finger-lickin' and cover-your-face-in-BBQ-sauce good.

MAPLE

The best kind of carb loading

**3418 11th Street NW (near Monroe Street NW) / +1 202 588 7442
dc-maple.com / Open daily**

Maple is a casual venture with a focus on food that pairs well with wine, aka heaven. Given that I am quite the oenophile, I can be found here often. It's marvelous for a get-together with friends, or a date, as the plates are all easy to share and meant to go with the several glasses of wine you'll down. Begin with a bruschetta sampler and be sure to order at least one of the tagliatelle pastas: both the lamb ragu and the mushroom truffle are absolutely delectable. Make sure to come here on your diet's cheat day, as Maple's toasted breads are dreamy. There's even a dessert bread, the Nutella panino, with Nutella, smashed banana and toasted hazelnuts. That one I won't be sharing.

REDROCKS NEAPOLITAN BISTRO

Tasty pizza and beers

1036 Park Road NW (near 11th Street NW) / +1 202 506 1402
redrocksdc.com / Open daily

Much to my eternal dismay, Washington is lacking when it comes
to pizzerias. Though Two Amys in Georgetown has its devotees,
RedRocks is where I go for a couple of slices and a good time. There are
a few outposts around the city, but the original is in Columbia Heights,
dishing out pies, panini and other Italian bites, and pouring from their
extensive selection of draft and bottled beers, wines and mixed drinks.
This is an excellent place for gathering a group of friends at a picnic table
on the enormous patio for a long, leisurely meal.

ROOM 11

Tipples and nibbles

3234 11th Street NW (near Lamont Street NW) / +1 202 332 3234
room11dc.com / Open daily

Once a dive, Room 11 has transformed into a multi-concept eatery and wine bar – but the real reason to go remains the drinks, and these days, the menus are focused around them. Room 11 serves seasonal small plates and scrumptious baked pastries to pair with its craft cocktails and carefully chosen wine list. The offerings change quarterly, with soups, salads and shareable appetizers like olives, cheese and charcuterie rotating often. I enjoy visiting on a cold winter's night to order a hearty soup, a gooey grilled cheese and an Old Fashioned. To finish things off, I love the apple cake, and have even been known to order more cheese if I'm feeling gluttonous.

THIP KHAO

Laotian street food with a cult following

**3462 14th Street NW (near Meridian Place NW) / +1 202 387 5426
thipkhao.com / Closed Tuesday**

I actually witnessed chef and owner of Thip Khao, Seng Luangrath,
win multiple food competitions — including a crab cake competition
I judged — before I gave her usual cuisine a try. Now, I regularly swing
by here for dinner. For appetizers, I always order the siin haeng, sun-dried
beef with ginger and sriracha sauce, and naem khao, lettuce wraps with
crispy coconut rice, lime, scallions, sour pork, peanuts and cilantro.
For mains, there's a variety of Southeast Asian soups, stews and curries,
and I wholeheartedly recommend the red curry. Thus far, I've enjoyed
everything I've sampled, which must mean it's time for a trip to Laos.

day tripping to alexandria

Hospitality and history in Old Town

Alexandria, or Old Town as it is affectionately known, is a little piece of Southern charm located across the Potomac River in Virginia, making it perfect for a day trip. Old Town's cobblestone streets are lined with historical buildings, seafood taverns, bakeries and cupcake shops, and — most importantly — fabulous boutiques. Though it's not so far that you have to make a day of it (a 40-minute Metro ride from central D.C.), there's enough to keep you occupied in Alexandria that it's possible to do just that. So take my advice and hit up the following to make the most of your time here.

First things first: brunch. Even if the food was middling (and it isn't), I'd dine at **Virtue Feed & Grain** because the space is so stunning. Built into an old granary, it offers up Southern comfort food, plenty of seafood (I love the lobster roll) and vegetarian-friendly options. Don't miss the mac and cheese, which includes gouda, havarti, Ritz cracker crumble and prosciutto lardons.

Once I've had my fill, it's time to shop. I like to start at **Mint Condition**, a bright consignment shop filled with designer goods from the likes of Tory Burch,

Lilly Pulitzer and Tibi to see if I can score an amazing steal. Then, I make my way to **She's Unique**. It's owned by a fashion blogger, so it only makes sense that the jewelry collection is well-curated, affordable and focused on layering. I personally love the bangles with geographical coordinates of popular cities and the stackable rose gold rings. After I've accessorized, I go to **The Shoe Hive**, a pricey, but fanciful women's store that isn't only about kicks: they also have jewelry and tights.

Now that I have myself a new outfit, it's time to outfit my place, which calls for a stop in **The Hour**. The store is dedicated to all things cocktail, and there's something for every whiskey girl and Martini devotee here. I can never resist splurging on something vintage for my bar cart. I also like swinging by **The Dog Park**, a shop hawking leashes, collars and clothes for pets.

After all that shopping, you're probably ready to eat again. Mosey over to **The Majestic**. Established in 1932, the restaurant cooks up delish American fare (I'm a huge fan of the shrimp and grits and the rockfish hush puppies) and strong drinks. A day done well, I'd say.

MINT CONDITION
103 South Saint Asaph Street (near King Street)
+1 703 836 6468, shopmintcondition.com
closed Monday

SHE'S UNIQUE
205 King Street (near North Lee Street)
+1 703 836 8863, facebook.com/shesuniqueva
open daily

THE DOG PARK
705 King Street (near North Washington Street)
+1 703 888 2818, thedogparkva.biz, open daily

THE HOUR
1015 King Street (near North Henry Street)
+1 703 224 4687, thehourshop.com
open Friday through Sunday

THE MAJESTIC
911 King Street (near North Alfred Street)
+1 703 837 9117, majesticcafe.net, open daily

THE SHOE HIVE
127 South Fairfax Street (near Prince Street)
+1 703 548 7105, theshoehive.com, open daily

VIRTUE FEED & GRAIN
106 South Union Street (at Wales Alley)
+1 571 970 3669, virtuefeedgrain.com, open daily